Alabama Village

Alabama Village

FAITH, HOPE, AND SURVIVAL IN A SOUTHERN TOWN

J. MALCOLM GARCIA

SEVEN STORIES PRESS

NEW YORK • OAKLAND • LONDON

Seven Stories Press
140 Watts Street
New York, NY 10013
www.sevenstories.com

Library of Congress Cataloging-in-Publication Data is on file.

ISBN: 978-1-64421-497-8 (paperback)
ISBN: 978-1-64421-498-5 (ebook)

College professors and high school and middle school teachers may order free examination copies of Seven Stories Press titles. Visit https://www.sevenstories.com/pg/resources-academics or email academic@sevenstories.com.

Printed in the United States of America

9 8 7 6 5 4 3 2 1

"But you should keep a clear mind in every situation. Don't be afraid of suffering for the Lord. Work at telling others the Good News, and fully carry out the ministry God has given you."

2 TIMOTHY 4:5

"When you hear two shots you think someone is testing their gun or something. Multiple shots, yeah, this is a shootout and they'll fire every bullet they have in every direction and not care who they hit."

DA'CINO DA'MARCUS DEES, Alabama Village

Contents

Prelude

For a short time, a photograph of Tony "TJ" Brisker hung alone above a white wood door at Light of the Village, a church in Alabama Village, a destitute neighborhood in the Mobile suburb of Prichard in southern Alabama. Other young men in the neighborhood had died violently before him; more than a few had combustible tempers, sold drugs, and toted guns, but they had mothers and fathers and siblings and in some instances children, and their families and friends missed them. The founders of the church, John and Dolores Eads, felt each passing. They had known almost all of them as children and although they did not condone many of their choices, they also believed that drug dealing did not define the entire person. They spoke at their funerals and mourned their absence. Because of how they lived, their deaths, although tragic, did not shock them.

TJ's death, however, did.

Since they began their ministry in 2002 in an abandoned crack house on Baldwin Drive in Alabama Village, John and Dolores had never seen TJ raise his voice in anger. Not once.

He didn't carry a weapon, and he never had an altercation with the police that they knew of—or with anyone else. The idea that someone would shoot him made no sense. Everyone liked him.

He was thirty years old and stood six feet, three inches tall. He had broad shoulders and thick, neatly cut, pitch-black hair. He maintained a tightly trimmed goatee and looked out at the world with an inscrutable gaze. He dressed casually in T-shirts of all colors and blue jeans. A jacket when the weather turned cold. Big TJ, the young people called him. He had seen his father shot and killed in a Mobile housing project when he was about fifteen. He rarely spoke about that or anything else. John and Dolores heard him say maybe six words in the years they had known him, in a voice whose pitch was higher than might be expected from a man of his size.

What up TJ?

Mmmm, he'd respond if he said anything at all.

He wandered around the Village like nothing else mattered, stopping at the church to shoot baskets on a court behind it. When guys got together for a game, TJ would join them without asking, without a word of any kind, and no one challenged him. He didn't dribble the ball or do any fancy footwork. He rarely moved at all. He preferred instead to stand in one spot swaying from side to side and watching the other players. The sun would beat down, sweat would wax his arms, and he would barely blink. He rocked back and forth as if listening to something beyond the hearing of the other players. They all knew not to leave him open because if he caught the ball he would score. Gripping the ball in his big hands, bent at the knees, his eyes narrowed, he would jump, releasing the ball in one fluid motion, his arms remaining in the air like a conductor until the ball whooshed through the net. He didn't run a victory lap or pump his arms or shout. He would stand motionless and solemn and begin swaying again, waiting to snag the ball. He never remarked upon his skill. If he couldn't make a shot, he passed the ball, but that rarely happened. TJ scored.

A small, shaggy, black terrier mutt followed him. Whether it was his dog or a dog that adopted him no one knew. He never spoke to the dog or called it by name, but they communicated in their way, the dog patiently staring at him, alert to the unspoken messages that passed between them. They were a pair, and the dog sat and waited for him when he went inside the church to ask for a basketball. Some people described TJ as simple. Other people presumed he was mentally retarded. John and Dolores never accepted such characterizations. They thought TJ was content, a man who took pleasure in his own company and that of his dog and expected or needed little in return.

He couldn't read, so Dolores set him up with a CD player and he listened to recordings of the Bible. Sometimes he would sit inside the church at a cubicle or outside at a picnic table under the shade of a tree, interrupted from time to time by falling acorns. He listened to the recordings at the basketball court while other young men played. On Sundays, he would attend John's Bible study class. He never asked questions or indicated if he had a favorite Gospel. When Dolores saw him, she would ask, Do you want to listen to the Bible? Yes, TJ would respond in that high, quiet voice of his, or if he saw her first he would say, Can I listen? and Dolores would give him the CD player with the Bible audiobook.

John and Dolores may have been one of the last friendly faces TJ saw before he died on a dank, drizzly December evening in 2011. They had been driving a white van filled with twenty bags of Christmas gifts for Village families. The headlights on low to cut through a dense, gray mist. The roads slick and wet. The van bumped over asphalt shattered by tree roots, almost impassable from decay and neglect. Wipers thumping back and forth. Dim illumination from the shuttered houses, weighted by weather, did little to beat back the gloom.

About six young men whom John recognized sprawled on the warped porch of TJ's home, a pale green house on Chilton Street not far from the church. A sagging strand of white Christmas lights framed the door. Recognizing John, the young men moved aside as he mounted the steps. Hey, Mr. John, they said. He stood before them holding a bag with a new pair of white sneakers and a box of chocolate cookies and asked for TJ. He's inside, they told him. John raised a fist and knocked on the door. He'd had a long day. The weather sucked. He had seventeen more presents to deliver. He wanted to finish this and drive home to Bay Minette about thirty miles away.

Just go inside, one of the young men told him.

John opened the door. Blue light from a TV illuminated the interior. Rumpled blankets on a living room couch suggested someone had used it as a bed. Dishes and glasses and foam food containers cluttered the kitchen counter. TJ emerged from the depths of a back hall.

Hey, we got gifts for you, John said.

He gave TJ the bag.

Check this out, TJ.

TJ cleared counter space for the cookies, withdrew the shoebox from the bag and looked inside.

Thanks, he said after a moment with no inflection to his voice, but John thought he was pleased.

This is great, TJ said.

Merry Christmas, TJ, John said.

Merry Christmas.

We'll see you Sunday.

Yeah, I'll be there.

TJ saw him to the door. John hurried out, wished the guys on the stoop a Merry Christmas. You too, Mr. John, they said as he got into the van. One down, sixteen more to go. The chilly night penetrated his coat and made him shiver. He turned up the heat. He and Dolores completed two more deliveries when he received a call from Key Key, the daughter of Betty Catlin, a church employee.

Hey, did you hear? Key Key said.

Hear what? John asked.

TJ. He died.

No! I just saw him.

Yes, he did too. I just got a call.

Are you sure?

He got shot, Mr. John.

John spun the van around and raced back to TJ's house. Yellow police tape cordoned off Chilton Street, snapping and wavering, and the rotating red lights from the roofs of squad cars bruised the surrounding homes and the faces of the gathered men and women, their voices hushed, curious. An ambulance had already taken TJ to Southern Alabama Medical Center in Mobile. When John and Dolores got there, he was in the ICU, brain-dead but on life support for organ donation. Eyes closed, a bloody bandage around his head. A tube in his mouth. Machines beeping, bright lights reflecting off a white tile floor and ceiling. John said a prayer, God be with TJ now and give him peace. His mother, whom John had met before but didn't know well, thanked him for coming. She told him TJ had shot himself. He was depressed, she said in a flat voice that revealed no emotion but John saw the pain in her sunken eyes.

He refused to believe TJ had died by suicide. He had not seemed unhappy when he saw him. John knew the young men on the porch carried guns. He thought it was more likely one of them had been playing with a pistol and killed TJ by accident. He couldn't imagine anyone shooting him on purpose. He couldn't imagine TJ doing it to himself.

He enjoyed going to the church, his mother said.

In the following days, TJ's death lingered in John's thoughts, a disturbing presence. He had been in a rush to deliver all of the Christmas gifts. He had left TJ's house too soon. He should have given him more time. Maybe he was depressed. Maybe he needed him and in his hurry John had not been sensitive enough to notice. He scolded himself: I was one of the last people he saw and all I could say was, Merry Christmas, see you Sunday, because I wanted to get home. He thought of how TJ enjoyed listening to the Bible. In his own way, he had been talking to God up until he died. This thought didn't deaden the pain of his death or of John's self-recrimination. However, it gave him perspective and a dose of humility. This wasn't about what he should or should not have done. It wasn't about him at all. It was about TJ. He had not died alone but in the comfort of his faith. Still, John thought, he should try to be a little more aware. The fragility of life in the Village meant that those he saw one day he might not see the next.

The photo John and Dolores picked to commemorate TJ showed him on a sunny day standing with boys who participated in recreational activities at the church. They were gathered before a blue-and-green mural with its white, puffy clouds and a black crucifix suspended in the sky with the declaration *Jesus Is The Way* below it. A few of the boys smiled. Others crossed their arms and flashed gang signs. TJ wore a white T-shirt. His hair caught the sun; his head was cocked a little to one side.

John and Dolores hung the picture without ceremony. For anyone who asked about it, they explained that at one time a man named TJ had come to the church accompanied by a small black dog and listened to the Bible and played basketball. He lived in the memories of those who knew him and also, John and Dolores believed, in heaven.

In the years that followed TJ's death, weeds, trees, and brush consumed Chilton Street, and many more young people died. The rising death count influenced John and Dolores to establish a memorial. TJ's photo and dozens of more pictures of mostly young black men who at one time had participated in the church now take up a wall. The majority of them, like TJ, were shot. The families of the deceased tape photographs of their loved one on the wall and John says a prayer. The photographs will remain as long as the church exists. A commemoration to the dead, a warning to the living.

Overture

December 2020. A friend calls and tells me about a feature story he saw on PBS about this neighborhood called Alabama Village. It is one of the most violent places in the country, the broadcast said. The show compared its strife to the civil war in Syria. When I lived in Illinois, people called Chicago *Chiraq*, because of its astronomical homicide rate—as many as forty shootings on some weekends. But that was Chicago. It was hard to believe that an obscure neighborhood in an equally obscure small Southern town would in its own way be as bad as Chicago, let alone the Syrian civil war.

I search the internet for more information. Prichard, a predominantly Black city of 19,322, according to the 2020 census, is among the poorest in Alabama, with a median household income of just over $36,000 and more than 30 percent of its population below the poverty level.

Prichard was incorporated in 1925, about five miles south of Mobile, and industrial development fueled growth in the city in the decades that followed. The community of Alabama Village was a war housing project within Prichard developed in 1942 for shipbuilders working in and around Mobile. Single-story homes, similar in appearance to enlisted housing on a military base, lined its streets, which were named after Alabama counties.

Following the war, the residences became available for private purchase; many of the workers from the nearby paper mills and shipyards bought homes here, and the white population in Prichard soared to about forty-seven thousand by 1960. Alabama Village thrived as a typical blue-collar community, offering permanent homes for many low-income families throughout the 1950s and '60s.

Property values began falling in the 1980s and crime began to rise, changes that coincided with white flight and the rise to power of Black politicians. By the 1990s, there were only a handful of families who owned and physically lived in their homes in the Village. Many property owners rented out their houses. Over time, however, collecting rent became difficult, and in some cases dangerous. Unable to sell, many landlords chose to abandon their property. The majority of them made their residences available for government-subsidized housing. Prichard suffered from declining tax revenues as businesses closed or moved. Between 1970 and 2014, the population declined 48 percent. The city's finances were depleted to such a point that in 2012, according to *The New York Times*, Prichard became the first municipality in the United States to stop making pension payments to retired city workers.

Crime continued to grow. In 2008, Prichard was listed as the eighth most dangerous city in the United States. The city's violent crime rate from 2001 to 2008 was higher than the state and national levels. From 2009 to 2012, the violent crime rate increased to 400 percent of the state and national rates. In 2013, the city of Chickasaw, which shares a border with Prichard, erected barricades across Iroquois Street, which used to link The Avenues, a working-class Chickasaw neighborhood, with Alabama Village.

Political corruption added to these problems. In 2019, former Prichard City Clerk Kim Green was accused of stealing more than $400,000 while working for the cities of Creola and Prichard. Prosecutors put Prichard's loss at $158,449. Mayor Jimmie Gardner said the city was blindsided by her guilty plea.

One year later, a judge sentenced James A. Blackman, a former chief of staff of Gardner's, for pocketing about $200,000 from Prichard between January and December 2017.

Predictably, city services suffered from neglect. Fire protection has been hobbled by low and undependable water pressure. In 2018, 93 percent of Prichard's fire hydrants failed an inspection. The Alabama Department of Environmental Management describes Prichard's water lines as being in dire need of repair.

With so many problems facing Prichard, the Village's predicaments festered. About forty-two families live in the Village today. City services barely exist. In the Village, about a million gallons of water once supplied to homes and businesses drains out of decaying pipes every year. The few remaining streets flood for days after a heavy rain because of the drinking water that collects in the storm sewers.

The Village may not be Syria, but its desolation and violence shocked me. I had been a social worker for fourteen years helping homeless people in San Francisco's Tenderloin district. They turned empty buildings into crash pads and crack houses. The hovels I had seen made me nauseous, but what I saw in the Village was on a scale beyond anything I'd ever experienced.

I made the jump into journalism at forty and devoted myself to covering families like my former homeless clients, people who live well below the news radar, and if in the unlikely or unfortunate event they become noteworthy, are generally viewed with disdain. The residents of the Village fell into that category.

I wonder about John and Dolores Eads. What is their motivation? As a social worker, I worked with religious people and found they did not stick around long when their prayers went unanswered. Too often they suggested the homeless men and women I worked with didn't have faith. John and Dolores, however, had stuck with it for twenty years. Surely, they've suffered disappointment. Surely, some of their prayers have gone unanswered. But they stayed. They had to be more than do-good Jesus people.

I call John on a Wednesday morning. Totally cool, he says when I tell him I want to write about the Village. I give him a little of my social services background, how my agency had to endure state budget battles and budget cuts. That's screwed, he says. Sounds like it sucked. Total crap. We don't accept government funding. He does not ask if I'm saved, as have other Christians I've met. He doesn't go there. I'm a stranger on the phone interested in his work. Nothing more, nothing less.

He explains that he and Dolores do not restrict themselves to a denomination. When they started Light of the Village, John wondered if he should study theology but a pastor at a Baptist church he attended in Mobile dissuaded him. For what God has called on you to do, do you think the kids care about a degree? No, John said. That settled it. John considers himself a layperson who practices his faith. If someone had to put a finger on it, he would say that he and Dolores are evangelicals. They take the Bible and go verse by verse, story by story, allowing it to speak for itself. They do not push it. They do not cram it. Anyone can come to the ministry. It offers free after-school programs, meals, and Bible study. Faith or lack of it has no bearing on who can participate.

I'm not selling a product, John tells me.

If I want to visit the Village, I'm more than welcome. He suggests people I should meet, including a guy he calls "Bigg Man." He's deep in the street but has good insight, John says. We've known him for years.

A magazine editor I know is enthusiastic about a story on the Village so in late February 2021, I throw my duffel bag into my car and leave my San Diego home for Alabama.

PART ONE

1

Miz Phyllis remembers.

Corey's momma, Sandra, her baby sister, a Davis too, lived a few houses down at 324 Baldwin Drive next door to the Cotton family and not far from where Mr. John and Miz Dolores built their church. Not far at all, God's truth. Miz Cotton, a little old lady, spent her days sitting on the porch in the shade of a poplar despite the sticky summer heat. Miz Phyllis would visit with her. The Cotton house, long gone as are so many other homes, the decline of the Village so obvious Ray Charles could see it. Overgrowth and ruin, vacant lots and collapsed houses. What truly remains resides only in Miz Phyllis's memory and the memories of others who have lived here as long as she has.

She leans forward, her face a warren of lines. Standing up, she draws the curtains to tamp down the heat from the sun, and the smell of cigarettes and the weight of musty odors settle in dark corners. She wipes her face with a washcloth. Flies buzz in the kitchen, bounce off the walls amid the rustle of a paper bag disturbed by a rotating fan.

Corey's momma, well, she liked to be in the street, Miz

Phyllis remembers in a voice strained by a cold. She'd leave baby Corey with her so often that Miz Phyllis ended up keeping him from the age of two until he got grown. Corey Davis was his given name but everyone—except Miz Phyllis—called him Bigg Man, even when he was small. He was a fat little boy with a cocky confidence that lent itself to the nickname. Lawrence, her son, and Bigg Man became like brothers. Bigg Man looked up to her daughter, Denise, like another momma. He had an older brother but he died at fourteen, struck twice by a car. He didn't have a chance, bless his heart. Going on twenty years now.

Miz Phyllis got into the drug game a long, long time ago and stayed selling crack until it occurred to her that everyone who had been out there with her was dead or in prison. She wasn't going to no prison and she wasn't in no hurry to die, so she walked away from the game. Not long after, she met Mr. John and Miz Dolores. No one could hardly miss them, a white couple like that in the Village—although she learned later Miz Dolores was Mexican, a pale one but Mexican all the same. Mr. John was all white, his hair blowing every which way when he wasn't wearing a cap.

In those days, Mr. John and Miz Dolores handed out hot dogs and organized games for children, Bigg Man and Lawrence among them, while they repaired the crack house that became their church. It took them a minute, but God blessed them and they fixed it up nice, to how it is now: White and bright as a smile with a big red cross outside, and they called it Light of the Village and it was.

Bigg Man and Lawrence tested Miz Dolores and Mr. John. Oh, they were bad boys. They jumped on their blue two-door Toyota pickup one afternoon and refused to get off. They were having so much fun playing games at the church they didn't want Mr. John and Miz Dolores to leave. Miz Phyllis saw them and shouted, I'm going to beat y'all if you don't leave off of their car! She picked up a stick and the boys bolted. Miz Phyllis didn't play, not then and not now, and they knew it. Let's get out of here! she heard Miz Dolores tell Mr. John and that little pickup leaped forward and got gone just like that. They always came back though.

As a boy, Bigg Man worked for the church cleaning yards. Got baptized too, by Mr. John at Spring Hill Baptist Church in Mobile. Coming up he was a good child until he started doing things he had no business doing. He stopped going to church but he never stopped believing in God or in Mr. John and Miz Dolores.

The streets schooled him. He snatched his first car when he was seven. It belonged to Miz Phyllis's brother. She can't recall the make but it was a nice ride. It was a sunny day, a good afternoon for driving. Miz Phyllis's brother tore his tail up, whooped him real good, but that didn't stop Bigg Man. At fourteen he stole a neighbor's car. The neighbor knew what he had done and was on him just that quick. Bigg Man drove it a few blocks before he stopped, ran out, and hid in Miz Phyllis's backyard. Miz Phyllis told him, Don't do that. Don't steal anybody's car, but he didn't listen. He never broke into houses; he was just a car thief. When he saw keys in a car he jumped on it like white on rice. Not even a teenager, so short at the time that his head didn't show above the steering wheel, and at first people thought the slow-moving car had no driver and had instead become possessed and taken over by spirits.

One of Bigg Man's homeboys, Alexander "Junior" Amerson, sold him a '96 Cadillac DeVille in 2019. Junior told him what he needed to do to keep it running. Two weeks later Bigg Man confronted Junior and called him all kind of names. Man, what the hell is wrong with this car, it just stopped running? What kind of gas you been putting in it? Junior asked him. Diesel. Bro, Junior said, when I sold it to you I said it takes premium gas. Bigg Man's face went blank. Damn, Junior, he said finally. They both busted out laughing and took it to the junkyard. Miz Phyllis still smiles whenever someone reminds her of that story.

Bigg Man did time in prison for marijuana possession in 2018 and that scared him. He played dice behind the walls and lost, and didn't have the money to pay his debts. The man he owed threatened to kill him, so Lawrence sent Bigg Man $150. He actually owed fifty dollars but the man charged him interest for being late. After he got out, he started loaning money to his homeboys to gamble and then he'd collect from them. You're crazy, Miz Phyllis told him. Shooting dice. Shooting craps. Just leave it alone. And stop flashing your winnings. Stop having that money on you like that. Give it to somebody or put it up. But he never would. He gets on Facebook and Instagram with tall stacks of twenty-, fifty-, and one-hundred-dollar bills. You can't go showboating on the internet, she warns him. These folks will feel all kinds of envy and hurt you. He never listens. Fast money's addictive. Miz Phyllis knows all too well. Too easy to get greedy, Bigg Man, she warns him, too easy.

Miz Phyllis understands people judge Bigg Man poorly, but they don't realize that when a child comes up in a certain area, they adapt. All Bigg Man saw were men in the street, older guys in their late teens and early twenties hustling and making money selling drugs. They raised him and Lawrence. That's what Bigg Man knew. That and the church.

She stands and opens the door to let in air. Sunlight bathes the living room, revealing a black couch, a worn brown carpet, and a large, flat-screen TV perched on a table cluttered with ashtrays. Outside, the sound of voices far off. Collapsed lawn chairs in the driveway. The smell of cut grass.

Miz Phyllis senses Bigg Man has grown tired of the street life. She did. The streets age a person but for now he's still out in them. Bigg Man is a twenty-four-hour hustler. He can lose it all in a dice game and two weeks later get it back. A hustler hustles. He's not a gangster. A gangster takes what they want. They watch other people hustle and try to take it from them. Miz Phyllis tells Bigg Man not to let just anybody into his circle, but he tells her the Village is his 'hood. It might be your 'hood, she reminds him, but everybody in your 'hood ain't for you. He won't hear that. He figures he knows everybody and everybody knows him. She thinks he is fooling himself. People can get to acting crazy. They get to feeling that they should have what he has. That he needs to be brought down to their level. But he doesn't listen; he won't be humbled.

I'm Bigg Man, he assures her.

2

Da'Cino Da'Marcus Dees wakes up in a house across the street from Light of the Village. John and Dolores recently bought the property and dubbed it the Lighthouse. They plan to use it for children who need a place to stay. Da'Cino will provide supervision. It has been completely remodeled. A little work still needs to be done—installation of cabinets and baseboards—but not much.

An old white man in his seventies, Gene Twiley, had owned the house before he moved to Florida in 2020. He had a thick head of graying hair and a beard and wore a cowboy hat, T-shirt, and overalls. He kept an owl decoy in his backyard because he thought it would scare away crows. Inside, the walls of the house were blackened by cigarette smoke.

He enjoyed sitting on the front porch but grew increasingly annoyed when young people traipsed across his property like he didn't exist. Mr. Gene, as he was known, put up no trespassing signs but most everyone ignored them. It was too easy to follow the cuts from Gulf Village, a housing project adjacent to Alabama Village, and saunter through his yard to Baldwin

Drive and up to Wilson Avenue, Prichard's main drag. Mr. Gene started toting a lever action .30-30 caliber rifle. People made sure he wasn't on his porch when they crossed his lawn. With the sanctity of his home restored, he grew to be pretty pleasant. He never entered the church, but he asked John to pray for his wife when she got sick with cancer. After she died, he donated odds and ends he found in his house including baseballs for the kids.

Da'Cino stands about six feet, four inches and keeps a beard cut to a thin line along his jawbone. He likes to wear T-shirts and gym shorts and flip-flops no matter the weather. A wide smile explodes across his face when he laughs. What up my boi! he shouts when he sees children at the church. He wants them to look at him as someone who lived through what they're experiencing and made it. Most people say no way when he tells them he's from Prichard. They think he has a Mexican name even though he's Black.

Before he moved into the Lighthouse, he had been spending nights with a sister in Gulf Village. He shared a bed with his nine-year-old nephew, Al. Al wasn't happy about it, but he didn't complain. Da'Cino didn't either but the kid thing drove him crazy. Man, the house could be so loud. His sister has five kids ranging in age from one to thirteen. In addition to them, she would also watch the children of her friends. Da'Cino would sit in his car after work until all the kids had gone to sleep. At least he had a place to lay his head. The subsidized housing he had lived in as a child was much worse. One house in particular had no water or electricity. He and his brothers and sisters heated bathwater on the grill his momma used to cook. Each of them washed in the same water until it was gray, soapy, and cold. His momma, Mary Dees, never renewed a lease, moving every year. Maybe she thought she'd get something better, something different. Da'Cino only knows that she never settled on one place for long.

Da'Cino grew up in the Village and was about eight years old when he first saw John and Dolores playing games with other children near the abandoned crack house. He was cutting grass with his stepdad, Joe. Da'Cino always worked. At first with Joe and then on his own when he grew older. He took his first job at Popeyes Louisiana Kitchen in Mobile when he was sixteen. At seventeen with the help of John and Dolores, he moved to Spanish Fort about twenty minutes away for a maintenance position at a movie theater. On his first day, the boss lady asked him, Do you know what you're supposed to be doing?

This, Da'Cino said, indicating the broom in his hand. Cleaning. I read the job manual.

Nobody ever reads that, she said, and promoted him to cashier. Over time he became shift leader and then manager. He stayed for six years until he accepted a job with the Wind Creek Casino in Atmore, about forty-five minutes from Prichard. Three years later, he became the manager of Premiere Cinema 14 Eastern Shore in Spanish Fort and moved back. John cosigned the lease for his apartment.

Da'Cino helped his cousin Junior get a job at the theater complex. One evening, a man complained about the sound in one of the theaters thirty minutes after the movie started. Why do y'all wait thirty minutes to tell us? Junior asked. He laughed in the man's face. The man asked to see the manager. Da'Cino found Junior and told him to wait for him in his office. He knew he had to do something. Junior was family and his homeboy, but he couldn't be laughing at paying customers. Da'Cino called John. You got to fire him just like anybody else who behaves inappropriately on the job, John told him. Da'Cino called his boss and asked to fire Junior. Permission granted. Junior was cool about it, but Da'Cino felt bad. After a few weeks, he helped him get his job back with the understanding he'd fire him again if he acted a fool.

Da'Cino lost his job and then his apartment at the start of the COVID-19 pandemic in 2020. He applied for jobs, but no employer responded to his resume. He began couch surfing between the homes of four sisters and volunteered at the church to fill his time.

Why don't you work for us? Dolores suggested one day. Come back tomorrow.

Da'Cino assumed she was joking and didn't return.

I thought you were going to work for us, Dolores said when she saw him again.

You were for real? Da'Cino asked.

The next day, he showed up.

He enjoys working at the church and playing with the kids, but the job never ends now that he lives across the street. After the church closes, people knock on his door at all hours, and they keep coming back, asking for food, clothes, and to use his phone. He'd prefer to live near Prichard, close enough to stay involved with John and Dolores but far enough away that people couldn't track him down after work. He didn't tell his homeboys and his family where he lived when he first moved to Spanish Fort. His momma would call when she was short on cash. You got twenty dollars so I can get a pack of cigarettes? He heard that so many times he lost count. He would tell her, I'm working, you know what I'm saying? I'll come and see y'all when I come to Prichard if y'all ain't busy.

No one gives him credit for nothing. When he bought a used

Toyota Camry, people said, Oh, the church got that for you. But it didn't; he bought it. He saved money and everything. His first car, a Honda Civic, John and Dolores helped him buy that. His momma will ask him, Call Mr. John and Miz Dolores for this and that. He never does. He won't beg for other people.

Why are these white people out here messing with kids? Da'Cino remembers wondering when he first saw John and Dolores. White people bought drugs in the Village and left. They didn't play with no children. Other church people had worked in the Village, but they always left. They couldn't meet the need, they said. Da'Cino thinks they didn't want to deal with the need.

It was weird. What is this? Da'Cino wondered. He didn't get it, white people all smiling and happy to be here. He wasn't happy. Why were they so happy? John stunned him when he walked over and talked to his stepdad and persuaded him to let Da'Cino join the other children. He couldn't believe he was having fun with white people at an abandoned crack house they were already calling a church. They wouldn't be here long, he assumed, like every other church. Black, white, it didn't matter. They all left. Maybe they were all about showing charity. Get their numbers up. Look at us. Look at how many people we're helping, but they weren't helping nobody. Not when they quit on them. He assumed John and Dolores would leave too. No way were these white people going to stay. Why were they doing this? What do they want? How long was this going to last? What made them want to be here? For years, Da'Cino asked himself these questions but he was reluctant to raise them with John and Dolores. He wasn't shy; he just didn't trust them because their presence didn't make sense. Sometimes Dolores approached him, and then he had to talk. It would just be the two of them. Dang, this short little white lady's going to want to talk, he thought. He never disrespected her but if she was speaking and Da'Cino's horseplay interrupted her, Dolores would pull him aside and look him dead in the eye, a smile on her face. She never got loud or mean. You know what you're doing, Da'Cino? Do you want to be disruptive? she asked a voice so soft it folded around him like licorice. He couldn't move. She wouldn't speak another word until he answered. She'd wait. Look at him through her big, round glasses. And wait. And wait. And wait. Until he finally spoke. He knew he better have the right answer or she would look so disappointed he'd want to cry.

In 2019, Da'Cino developed a staph infection. He couldn't bend the fingers in his left hand. He didn't know how he contracted the infection. His arm just started swelling one day. He went to three emergency rooms and each one dismissed the problem as tendonitis. This ain't no tendonitis, not with my arm this big, Da'Cino told himself. The doctors at a fourth ER agreed and rushed him into surgery. John and Dolores stayed with him the whole time. His momma, brothers, and sisters never visited.

Da'Cino has his duties. On this morning, a Sunday, he wakes up to open the church for Bible study. After he dresses, he sorts through a thick ring of keys before he leaves the Lighthouse and unlocks the security door to the church. Stepping inside, Da'Cino walks through a door to the kitchen. He takes a stack of paper cups from a cabinet and sets them on the counter. He finds packets of Kool-Aid, tears them open and pours them into a yellow cooler and adds cold water and ice. Sets the cooler on the counter beside the cups.

He turns on lights illuminating yellow cinder-block walls covered with photographs of families who attend the church. Some of the smiling men, women, and children wear blue Light of the Village T-shirts. One of them, Marion "Mayo" Awudu, a young man with dreadlocks, has a goofy grin. He was shot in 2019. Next to his photo, a picture of Cindy Darrington, a longtime church participant. She died in 2020. Her oldest son, Jesse, attends a community college. She would be pleased. She always wanted her children to have an education. Other photographs show spent bullets, a splintered window, a shell casing, reminders of where John and Dolores built their church. Keeping it real, Da'Cino has heard John say in Bible study. We can never forget where we are.

The door opens and Da'Cino turns toward Betty Catlin. She wears a gray T-shirt and blue jeans. Gold coloring streaks her hair.

Hey, Miz Betty, Da'Cino says.

Hey, Da'Cino. What's going on?

She walks behind the counter and glances around the stove.

You got some grease over there across the street?

No, Da'Cino says. I use the microwave. I cook everything in it. Don't need no grease.

That ain't cooking, Miz Betty tells him. I learned to cook from my momma and having six children. That'll do it every time. Yesterday I cooked steamed crab claws for the first time. Came out good.

You have garbage bags?

Right there in the pantry. To your left. Look and ye shall find.

Da'Cino laughs. Miz Betty cooks breakfast every Sunday morning: scrambled eggs, sausage, grits, and buttermilk biscuits. She serves anyone who drops by. Some people stay for the eleven o'clock Bible study; just as many leave after they eat.

At one time Miz Betty, her kids, and Da'Cino's family lived across the street from one another in the Prichard Homes housing project before they all moved to the Village, where Miz Betty rented a house in an alley and Da'Cino's momma lived nearby on Dekalb Street, known as D block. Da'Cino was always at Miz Betty's house. Then his momma moved them out of the Village into another part of Prichard and he didn't see Miz Betty as much. His momma stopped hanging with people like she had. She used to hang with everybody.

My momma and her boyfriend are beefing again, Da'Cino says, shaking coffee into a coffee filter. When she drinks liquor, they fight. She won't drink beer because it makes her pee. Now she's hanging with her sister. I didn't know there were that many kids over there. I was trying to figure out whose kids are whose. My cousin has like seven kids.

Miz Betty removes a pan from a cabinet and a large carton of eggs from the refrigerator.

And your cousin's momma has nine? she says.

Yes. Hey, what was the name of that girl who died?

Who? The one on the news?

She was fourteen and on crack.

That white girl? Miz Betty says.

Yeah, she died.

How long was she on crack?

I don't know. Ended up taking her to the hospital and pumping her stomach but she died. They said she ran away, hooked up with this dude, came back, and this happened.

You know what? Miz Betty says. My little cousin Angie, her and her family moved to Montgomery and she hooked up with this dude and he had her and this other girl prostituting. He beat her up so bad knocked an eye out of its socket. She's blind now. I mean, she can see but not good. Angie was like seventeen. I said, Who did that to your eye? She said, Nobody. I said, Nobody? You ain't fixin' to live with him, are you? You end up dead if you do. He almost beat her to death. Two weeks later, her and her momma moved back to Mobile. She said to me, Cousin, you was right.

You was.

You talk to Mr. John today?

Not yet.

Miz Betty breaks two dozen eggs into a glass bowl and throws the shells into a trash can. She whips the eggs into a froth. She has known John and Dolores since the first day she saw them in the Village. They got out of their car and within minutes had all these kids around them. If children liked them, they got to be alright, she remembers thinking. They stopped at her house off Barbour Drive and introduced themselves.

She was born in Mobile but her family moved to the Village in the early 1980s after her grandmomma passed and the family took over her house. Her momma used drugs and spent much of her time on the street. Her daddy drank and lived with his momma. In those days, Alabama Village had stores and houses on every block. Miz Betty used to go to dances at a gym. As an adult, she moved around the Village from one Section 8 house to the next. She lived on Blount Drive, Colby Street, Fayette Street, and Dekalb Street. She changed homes constantly because she wanted a better house. She had a cousin in a Mobile high-rise. He stuffed trash bags into holes in the wall. Landlords should be ashamed. As far as Miz Betty's concerned, if a tenant ain't behind on their rent, a landlord should fix their house.

At fifteen she had the first of five children. If she could go back in time, she would tell herself to wait. Just wait, girl. But she didn't. Only so much she can do now. Looking back doesn't change what's done. She talks to young people. Hey, come on here and let me holla at you. You ain't got no business hanging out like this. She pulls them aside and gives them something to think about. Other mothers look away: She ain't my child. I don't care about her. But not Miz Betty. Somebody's got to care about them, otherwise they'll be pregnant and become mothers way too soon, and then they'll see how hard life can be. It ain't about not having enough money. It's about wondering every day if your child will come home. Their fathers are out and up to no good. It's the mothers who get the calls. One night, Betty's phone rang and the girlfriend of her son Carlos told her he was dead. Miz Betty's heart dropped so far she could feel it hit the floor and her chest ached with every breath. But the girlfriend had been mistaken. It was another young man who had died.

Miz Betty likes where she lives now, a neighborhood in the northern part of Mobile called Crichton. It's a little more restful than the Village. She still hears gunshots but less often. In the

Village, it was every day. Or there would be fights. Everybody
wanted to meet in a field and have at it. Y'all bring your problems over here and we get all the heat, she scolded them. Look
at these older people on their porches trying to relax. They
ain't paying no bills to look out over a field and watch you
fools fight. Girls with their children in their boyfriends' cars
watching them go at it like it was a basketball game. Scar their
children for life. Betty shakes her head. It's no wonder children
turn out as they do.

On Facebook people asking for bail money for AJ.

What he do?

Shoot someone, Da'Cino says.

Young AJ?

Not that AJ you talking about, Miz Betty. He doesn't do
anything. I'm talking about another AJ. He's older.

They got him?

Arrested him.

AJ the rapper? Miz Betty says Who does the beats?

No, that's young AJ. This is another AJ.

Another?

Yeah. They caught him, Da'Cino says.

That's crazy.

Miz Betty pours Crisco oil into a pan, heats and lifts the pan,
tilting it, rolling the oil around. Setting it back on the stove,
she spreads round sausage patties on the bottom of the pan.
Oil spits and hisses. Miz Betty dials down the flame. She places
a sheet of biscuits in the oven and sets the temperature at 425
degrees.

So far my sister's boyfriend is somewhat normal, Da'Cino
says. He has a job. He works and draws a check from the government too.

His job is probably paying him under the table.

They got married, so she's not on Section 8. They're paying their rent but they're paying more than Section 8. I said, Why'd you get married? He was staying with you anyway. It's not going to change. Except now you got a ring.

All they got to do is separate, and she'd be back on Section 8, Miz Betty says.

I don't think she'll do it. They drove three hours away to get married, I know that.

So they're not even in the system. That's why a lot of people in Mobile go to Mississippi: So their marriages aren't registered here and they can get Section 8.

If you get married, you should be in a home, Da'Cino says. Not staying in government housing.

With a yard, a garage, and a house—like a for real house.

The sausage sizzles. Miz Betty flips the patties with a spatula. Da'Cino glances at the clock and leaves to arrange a room for adult Bible study. Chairs stacked against a wall. He removes two folding tables from the room and carries them into the hall, collapses the legs and leans them against a wall. Then he arranges the chairs in five rows with five chairs in each row.

Everyone knows Da'Cino as Cino from the church. His mind gets all twisted—trying to be an example, living across the street but not being part of the 'hood. Who am I? he wonders. He has homeboys who hang out and sell drugs but he never joins them. They do their thing, and he does his. He doesn't tote a gun. He's never been to jail, not even close. He's about to turn thirty. That shocks him. He feels old thinking about it and wishes he could remain younger instead of growing older, but it beats the alternative. Many of his homies never reach their mid-twenties. When he was little, older people in their thirties ran the streets. Now, he's their age and it's all younger people walking the blocks. Back in the day, people didn't shoot in broad daylight like they do now. As a child, he could go outside. But even in those days, he had to be situationally aware. He never knew that expression until he heard Mr. John use it. No one told him, 'Cino, don't go there. He just knew, like instinct passed from one generation to the next. Like how wild animals run from people because they know they'll be shot. Instinct. Sometimes he gets a bad feeling like it's a cloud blocking the sun, and in the shadow of that feeling he thinks, Yeah, I'm not going over that way. The uneasiness comes from something he can't define but it tells him to get out, almost as if he's hearing voices. But he doesn't hear voices. It's just a presence that warns him. Instinct. Or ghosts of people already dead—but he doesn't believe in ghosts. It's his call to listen to it or ignore it. He listens. The presence never lies, and he's still alive. If he hears two gunshots, that's just normal. But if he hears multiple shots, he worries. That presence creeps up on him. Two shots? He assumes someone is testing their gun. Multiple shots? It's a shootout and they'll go through every bullet in the magazine, and it doesn't matter who they hit. Sometimes, they start shooting as they pull out their guns and blast their own feet.

He was eight years old when he saw his first shooting. He and his brothers, Marco and Jamichael, and their stepdad, Joe, watched a man chase and shoot another man in front of a Prichard convenience store on a sunny afternoon when the only other sound was traffic. Smoke flashed out of the shotgun and Da'Cino's legs turned to noodles. He had gone to the store on his scooter but after what he'd just seen, he couldn't move. The ambulance took a while to arrive, and the wounded man bled out in front of the store. The store owner wouldn't let him inside. He didn't want blood on the floor. Joe shouted to Da'Cino and his brothers, Y'all get over here! And they ran to a store across the street and bought what they needed. Joe acted no more out of sorts than he would have if the first store had been closed. That night, Da'Cino refused to go outside. He didn't want to walk into any surprises.

Shootings happen so often in and around the Village, he has stopped keeping track. Nothing minor about a dude shooting a gun; it's heavy, but he's been around it so many times that he knows how to react so people don't know that he's reacting at all. His legs still turn to noodles but he doesn't acknowledge his fear. If he feels too much, he'll break down. He'd be crying all the time. Everybody would be like that. He doesn't know where that jolt of surprise and fear goes. Somewhere. It gets diluted somehow and drains away and something else replaces it—something cold and blank that allows him to respond calmly so that he moves past his fear without dwelling on it, stuffs his feelings down deep where he can't reach them or hopes he can't. The effort leaves him exhausted like he has been on his feet all day.

He sleeps through shootings. Not always, but most times. You didn't hear that last night? No, Da'Cino will say, what happened? He gets used to it. Well, not used to it. Something else. He incorporates shootings into his life. Like eating and sleeping. Oh, someone's shooting; give me a Coke and some of those fries. He can't summon the fear he felt when he was a child and saw the man die in front of the convenience store. He remembers that moment but he no longer feels it.

After he finishes arranging the chairs, Da'Cino drops a black Bible on each one. He sets a red Bible on the lip of a white-board for Mr. John and then returns to the kitchen.

How many kids Jerome got? he asks Miz Betty.

Deborah Lacey's Jerome? Too many. Most of the kids in the Village is his.

Their mommas bring them to church.

Everybody know him as the daddy of all these kids.

Yeah, Da'Cino agrees.

I put two mousetraps down Thursday.

I see mouse droppings here.

You remember that bag of food we was looking for the other day? The mice went through it, Miz Betty says.

One of them is dead.

Maybe the food was bad.

What kind of food are we buying?

Miz Betty laughs, checks on the biscuits, removes them from the oven.

———✀———

A gray 2011 Prius with decals of the American and New Mexico flags and Airborne wings turns onto the grass in front of the church raising a flurry of flies and dust. Two dogs on Baldwin start barking, stop, and then trot into the woods, and the silence that had been present all morning returns. John and Dolores get out of the car followed by a teenager, Jamez Montgomery, who they picked up in Mobile. He has been with the church since he was five and lives with his grandmomma Deborah Lacey, the momma of his uncles Jerome and Mayo.

John and Dolores carry boxes of oranges and grapefruit that a friend gave them to distribute in the Village after church. Jamez follows them inside.

What up, Bo? John shouts.

What up, Bo? Miz Betty says.

John walks behind the counter and scoops up a sausage patty and slips it in a sliced biscuit. He calls almost everyone Bo—men and women, boys and girls, sparing himself embarrassment when he forgets a name. He has been saying Bo for so long now that everyone calls him Bo.

What's the word, Bo?

You got it, Bo, Da'Cino says.

John considers the dozens of photographs on the walls. One shows Da'Cino wearing a yellow T-shirt and flashing gang signs. Goofball, John thinks. Da'Cino wouldn't hurt a soul. As a kid, Da'Cino smelled so bad. His family never had running water. They'd go for months without water.

John remembers an afternoon when he and Da'Cino handed out flyers for a Thanksgiving meal at the church. There were many more houses in the Village then—not in good shape but still livable. It was like a scene in a movie. Da'Cino pointed to a cluster of men John had spoken to. The guy on the left, that's my dad, Da'Cino said. My real dad. John didn't know what to say. Da'Cino laughed. That's what he does when he feels uncomfortable, laughs off the pain. His father never came around and his mother kept to herself and let the stepdad control the house. Da'Cino can be very dismissive of his mother but he always visits her. John presumes he wants her love as much as any other kid. His father's too, probably. A child's need for their parents doesn't end because they have become adults or because their parents denied them affection. The desire to be loved doesn't disappear with age. There is a constant yearning, John thinks.

Da'Cino didn't hit it off immediately with John and Dolores. He was always very polite but he hardly spoke. Dolores would give him a ride home and play music, and he would just whisper along with the songs. At the church he seemed to have fun, playing tag, football, basketball and just hanging out. John would take him and his brothers out to mow grass and then he would buy them something to eat. Over time he spoke a little more. As a teenager, Da'Cino needed a place to live because his mother was moving across town, and Da'Cino wanted to remain involved with the church. With his mother's permission, John and Dolores placed him with a couple from the Village they knew and trusted. They bought Da'Cino a cell phone so they could check up on him. The phone took their status way up in Da'Cino's eyes. His joy turned into pranks. He'd call and say, Hey, meet my uncle, Uncle Click, and hang up.

Da'Cino occasionally refers to John as his godfather. John appreciates the compliment but he doesn't endorse it and respectfully corrects him. Thank you but I'm not. He is more like an uncle, a visiting relative. Someone who sees Da'Cino and other church participants and then leaves for the drive home to Bay Minette. John wants to avoid being sucked into something manipulative: You're like my dad, give me some money. Not the end of the statement. That's a comma, not a period. They want something behind the praise. Call him cynical but he has been doing this work for more than twenty years. He won't be used. They have their own fathers and mothers. He can't be them. During the Thanksgiving and Christmas seasons, he encourages everyone to say something nice to their mothers. They are still their mothers, flaws and all, and those flaws didn't materialize out of nowhere. They had their trials. If their fathers stayed involved, say something nice to them too. And even if they didn't. They too had their trials. Forgiveness is love.

Supporters of the church have told John: You and Dolores let Da'Cino stay across the street for free, he should show gratitude. John understands why they think that, but Da'Cino will never express his appreciation the way others would expect. He won't ever say, Thank you for letting me live here. But whenever John needs him, Da'Cino is available. So when someone says he should be grateful, John can only agree and leave it at that. He gets what they mean but he doesn't expect anything nor should he. He doesn't work in the Village for gratitude but to fulfill as best he can God's Word as he understands it. So many of the church participants have never known love. When they experience it, they take and take and take before it's gone, because they have not known anyone who gave and stayed.

Now after all these years, John and Dolores feel a part of the community. At first, the Village intimidated them. Still kind of does. They don't want to ever be complacent. The families here know them, but that only carries them so far. All they have to do is be in the wrong place at the wrong time and say the wrong thing or look at someone the wrong way and it's over. Period. Just like that.

—⁓—

An old photograph on the wall near the one of Da'Cino shows John and Dolores in front of the church years earlier with nine kids clustered around them. What year, John asks himself? Two thousand four, maybe? One boy peers over John's left shoulder, his arm draped across John's chest. Bigg Man when he was about eight years old.

John looks at Mayo's photo. He could be so silly, and loud. Mayo could be heard a block away. He always had this sleepy half smile on his face. He liked to knock on his neighbor's door every morning on Hale Drive and stare through the screen door without speaking, his long hair framing his face, just to mess with her. One day she wanted breakfast from Whataburger off Wilson Avenue but she didn't have enough money. Mayo said, Well you go up there and I'll get you and me something. She thought he was playing. He said, Are you ready or what? Are you going? She said, You for real? Yeah, I'm for real. And he bought them both breakfast.

He rarely got mad and when he did he never stayed angry for long. He played basketball, teased the other kids on the court, and called them sorry. He spent his days on Hale Drive or on Fayette Street in the Village. Hale was a big hangout spot.

One summer, when Dolores and John held a Bible camp, Mayo's older brother, Jerome, got into a car wreck. Mayo must have been about fourteen. Jerome almost died. Mayo asked Dolores, Can you talk to him about God? He brought him to the ministry, his face all messed up because of the accident. Mayo loved his brother and was afraid for him. Mayo told Dolores his brother wanted to learn about Jesus.

For a few weeks he had a job at a Mobile motel working security. His first job, a real job. A homeboy got it for him. He was happy but he didn't last but a week. He was busted smoking weed.

Mayo died in 2017. Twenty-six years old. Shot in his yard on Hale Drive. A memorial of faded purple, and green plastic flowers marks the spot where he fell, his name painted in pink letters on a board beside a fallen candleholder. The ministry held an evening memorial service for him behind the church.

A cross of candles flickered from the ground illuminating the night. Everyone said a little something. John remembered when Mayo was fourteen and participated in a field trip to a water park. He couldn't swim and used an inner tube. He wore it even when he stood in line to buy a hot dog.

You're at a snack bar, John told him.

I know, Mayo said, but I ain't letting this go.

After everyone spoke, they released balloons into the air.

John thinks Mayo died after getting into it with somebody and humiliating them in a battle of words. An audience of homeboys probably rode the dude hard.

Yeah, Mayo got you. Played you, man.

So the dude responds:

I'll get him.

And he did. Upped his street cred by shooting the man who humiliated him. Death has as much of a presence in the Village as the people living here, attaches to them like a second shadow. When John hears the *pop, pop, pop* of a gun, his mind flashes with questions: Where's this going? Is it someone just testing his weapon or something worse? After twenty years in the Village he has not grown used to the violence and doesn't want to, but he works with so many children who have. He recalls one April afternoon in 2014 when he stopped in Gulf Village to pick up the three Darrington boys, Jesse, Jeremiah, and Jerel, for an after-school program. Jeremiah got in the front seat. Every kid wants the front seat. Their mother, Miz Cindy, walked outside, spoke to John, and left just as two men running between houses began shooting at each other. A driver behind John jumped out of his car and ran. John could not back out. He reached over to push Jeremiah's head down, but he was already on the floor as were Jesse and Jerel. John was the only one sitting up, exposed. He dropped down and counted thirteen shots. Then the shooting stopped. Wind stirred. The absence of noise seemed louder than the gunfire. John absorbed the stillness settling around him until Jeremiah sat up, broke out a juice box, and stuck a straw in it.

OK, Mr. John, he said. We can go now.

They are all likable, the killers and the victims. John enjoyed Mayo but no one outside of his family thinks about him now. The same people who believe Da'Cino should express gratitude say Mayo got what he deserved. He brought it on himself, living as he did. He wasn't the worst of them. Bigg Man posts photos of himself with stacks of money on Facebook and Instagram. What do they expect? It's no secret what can happen flashing cash, running in the streets, but did Mayo or anyone else deserve it? Did Mayo ask for it? Is Bigg Man asking for it? John doesn't think so. A lot went into making Mayo who he was. John doesn't apologize for him, but it's too dismissive to say he asked for it.

Bigg Man is twenty-five. He was always into cars. The first few he owned weren't in great shape. Old beaters. Then one day he started driving really nice cars. Not something he fixed up himself, for sure. John and Dolores didn't ask questions. What would be the point? To turn him in? John thought about it but decided that if he and Dolores wanted to play a role in Bigg Man's life why would they do that? They'd never see him again. Then what would they have accomplished? They understand he's not on Wall Street. Bigg Man knows they know what he does. They don't talk about it directly, but Dolores always tells him to be careful. He appreciates the risks. John used to assume once a kid had seen someone shot, they'd do anything to avoid that outcome for themselves. He couldn't have been more wrong. They see the dangers, maybe they understand them, but they stay anyway. This is how life is.

John won't hesitate to contact the police if necessary. He does not excuse drug dealing. Do the crime, do the time. But the cops know what's happening, so who should he call? Is it better that he and Dolores set an example by the way they live and through their faith, hoping that what they're doing compels some of the people they see, old and young alike, to consider options other than the street? He has no pat answers. People avoid the Village for understandable reasons but what right do they have to pass judgment if they drive past Prichard without a thought other than some holier-than-thou criticism, some cloying cliché? Come here to the church and push a kid on a swing. Come back, push that same kid on a swing again, get to know them. Watch them grow. Experience their disappointments. Experience your own in them. They will disappoint; they most certainly will. No matter. It's all good. Keep coming back. Love that kid without conditions despite the disappointments. Feel them love you because you stayed, and feel yourself love them back even though you may not want to. You know each one of them could end up like Mayo, and if, God forbid, they do, try to make sense of it. Ask yourself: Did they deserve it?

3

Miz Betty scoops scrambled eggs onto paper plates, adds sausage and a biscuit, and hands the plates to Da'Cino, who places them on the counter for the families lining up. Children run outside to a playground beside the church, climb up a slide, or plop down on a swing, spilling their food. Dolores wends her way through the crowd, greets everyone by name. Hey! she shouts as if she hadn't seen them in weeks. She notices new faces and misses some of the old. A lot of young people stop attending Bible study after they become teenagers. She worries that she will lose her connections with them as they get older, that she will never know what happened to them.

At eleven o'clock, Dolores rings a cowbell announcing Bible study will begin soon. Adults continue talking and eating; the children keep on with their games. Dolores continues ringing the bell and slowly—and reluctantly for the children—people move in to an adjacent building and sit on the folding chairs Da'Cino arranged earlier, Bibles on their laps. Dolores stands at a podium and looks at them and the chatter subsides. She closes her eyes, folds her hands, and prays. She thanks God for the breakfast Miz Betty prepared and asks for guidance as they prepare to discuss one of the Gospels for the next hour. When she finishes, she asks preteen children to stand by a wall near the door. After they shuffle into place, she leads them back to the main building where breakfast was served and instructs them while John stays behind and conducts a class for adults and teenagers.

What up Caleb? John says, looking at one sixteen-year-old boy staring back at him. Caleb shrugs and smiles. He lives with his mother and works at Subway, a fast-food restaurant, in Mobile. Bought a used 2001 Ford Crown Victoria recently for $3,000 dollars. Bright green with more than one hundred thousand miles. Saved months for it but he didn't know to check the oil and blew the engine. Car sits in a junkyard now. Poor kid. It never occurred to John that he had no one in his life to teach him how to maintain a car. John doesn't know how much money Caleb owes the dealer but he will help him pay the balance.

BJ, all good, Bo? Straight up, OK. Before we begin, we what? Pray.

We pray.

John takes off his cap and slaps it against his right leg. He paces, looking down at the floor, speaking like someone thinking aloud to a companion.

Heavenly Father, we thank you for all the young people here. Not to serve us but to serve you. Help us learn from this Bible lesson. Something we can read, something we can listen to, but most importantly something we can hold on to.

He slaps his cap against his leg a final time and concludes, In Jesus's name we pray. Amen.

Amen!

Alright now are there any questions before today's lesson.

No, a boy shouts.

I didn't ask you, Corry. I appreciate your enthusiasm though. Any questions? OK, let's get to it. How many Gospels are there?

Twelve!

That's how many apostles there are. Gospels are the books of the New Testament. How many are there?

Four.

Matthew, Mark, Luke, and . . .

John.

Alright. OK, we're going to jump into Luke, chapter 14. We cool with that, all good so far?

OK. At the start of chapter 14, where is Jesus? He's on his way to Jerusalem. We know that from chapter 9. That's when he starts off. What's he going to do in Jerusalem? What? Yep, you're right, he's fixin' to go eat. What else is he going to do? He's going to die. OK. He's going to die for what? Our sins. Exactly right. So that's why he's on the road. Before we go to chapter 14, we need to rewind that tape a little bit and start with chapter 13 to remind ourselves a little bit about what we learned last week. Who wants to read?

John waits for a volunteer. He never asks someone. They may not know how to read and he doesn't want to embarrass them. Long ago he learned to assume nothing. He thinks the teenagers understand faith. They've learned about God growing up and many have attended a church at some point. They've heard the stories. How much the Bible influences their lives, John doesn't pretend to know. He has them for only a short time and does what he can to arouse their curiosity.

A girl raises her hand. Shalanda, go for it, John says. As she reads, the sun shines on the Memorial Wall. John has seen families press their fingertips against the pictures as if to feel those lost yet still loved, skin against skin, pulse against pulse. They say their names: George "Boo Face" Paige III was a Davis. He got shot by his cousin over a woman or four dollar, no one seems to know for sure. Antrell "Bam" Nichols. He was shot during an attempted robbery. Canzio. She got sick and died. Last name, Robinson. Everyone called her Red although not her hair or anything else about her was red. Sweet girl. She's gone all the same. Just got sick and died. Detoria Cook. She got shot in the head. Dorne "DJ" Wheeler, Jr. got killed. Someone shot him near a church down by Telegraph Road. There's Corey Jr., Bigg Man's son. He died of a gunshot wound in 2020. No more than a toddler. Gone just like that.

It's sad, John thinks. So many are gone. The list goes on.

When Bible study concludes, John and Dolores drive kids home who don't have a ride. After they drop them off, they return to the church and stack the boxes of oranges and grapefruit they had brought and load a white pickup. Da'Cino and Jamez help. The wind carries the sound of a freight train. Blue jays call, imitating a child's plaint. The sun beats down, trash is lifted from the ground by a swirling wind.

My birthday's tomorrow, Mr. John, Jamez says. Can I drive?

You ain't driving.

I'll be fifteen.

Now you sure ain't driving.

John backs onto Baldwin Drive, jostling on the pitted road.

He drives a short distance, turns onto Barbour, and crosses Dunlap Circle, rolling to a stop beside a row of battered white houses that are shedding peeled paint. Bits of paper swirl across the road and dogs disturb a cluster of foam food containers. An old man watches the pickup from behind a screen door, his worn face filled with questions.

We got oranges and grapefruit, Bo, John shouts at him.

That you, Mr. John? I'll take a few.

Alright, Bo.

Thanks, Mr. John.

See you later, Bo!

The pickup dips through water-filled craters, past a greenhouse shrouded in vines. The solemnity of its closed doors and shuttered windows suggest it has been deserted for years. However, at night it opens as a hit house and stands in a block John calls the Donut Shop, an area used 24/7 by drug dealers. Like a donut shop, it never closes, John says. Shirtless young men in sagging blue jeans pause, watch him pass through. Boom boxes blast static. Chained dogs send up a cacophony of barking.

Bingo, what's up, man? Want some fruit? Just off the tree.

I see the leaves on it, Mr. John.

That means it's fresh, Bo. Are you doing well?

Yeah.

John drives on. Boarded windows covered with warped plywood. Crushed aluminum cans clotted with flies. Discarded tires and broken bricks in heaps amid shards of broken glass. The bare ground is strewn with rocks. Beer bottles hang from the fingertips of those too intoxicated to drink more.

See Bigg Man? John asks Da'Cino. He motions with his chin toward a young man behind the wheel of a red Dodge Charger R/T. He wears a red sweat suit, a knit cap perched on his head.

He fills the car, one arm out the window, the other around the back of the passenger seat, and stares out the windshield at the activity around him like the supervisor of a work crew.

I like your car, Bo, John shouts to him. You ain't in the black one. You got more cars than General Motors.

He jumps out and offers him a sack of oranges. Bigg Man thanks him, stays in his car, engine running.

You good, Bo? John says.

Awright, Bigg Man says.

A man with a blue bandana wrapped around his head hurries toward the pickup as John gets back in. John knows him well: Bodine, the Village barber.

Where were y'all? I came to the church this morning, Bodine shouts, pretending to be annoyed but his eyes show his mischief.

We were there, John says.

I was there at nine.

We don't start till ten thirty.

I left and went out for breakfast. Had to spend fifteen dollars 'cause you wasn't there.

Had to, John repeats, not hiding the sarcasm in his voice.

Bodine laughs, grabs a sack of oranges. He learned to cut hair by experimenting on himself when he was fifteen. He faced a mirror and set up two other mirrors behind his head. He did a good enough job that his cousin and some friends asked him to cut their hair, and his business started. He draws pretty well too. Anything he sees, he can draw it. He doesn't charge much.

When John and Dolores first came to the Village, people would ask them to pay for their haircuts. John soon realized they did not always use the money as intended. He suggested to Bodine that they create a coupon. John would give the coupon to someone who wanted a haircut and then pay

Bodine for each coupon he collected. Bodine agreed, and they have worked together ever since.

Next week, come at ten thirty, John tells him. Have breakfast with us.

Bodine waves. John continues down Hale Drive, turns onto Escambia Street. Water covers part of the road and the truck slows to a crawl, rocking forward as the pickup eases into and out of one pothole after another. An open door of a vacant house reveals a doll's head on the floor and behind it an unhinged screen door. The walls and the roof have fallen around it and the branches of a tree compete for airspace with a brick chimney that stands sentinel over the rubble.

What did this used to be? Jamez asks, pointing to a cluster of white empty buildings concealed behind trees. A broken sign at the entrance of the driveway on rusted posts still promotes what had once been here.

Restoration Youth Academy. A boot camp, juvenile boot camp, John says. It closed in 2012. A homeless man, Tommie Bonner, better known as Mr. Tommie, lives there now.

Me and my friends went around there once. There were a whole bunch of dogs and they chased us. Used to be floods out this way didn't it, Mr. John.

Yeah, it used to flood. Still does.

A man walking alone on the road with his shirt open turns and faces the pickup, a hand raised to shield his eyes from the sun. The shiny remains of an otherwise charred truck reflect the midday glare. Piles of garbage fill an empty street that dead-ends into brush. Dogs trot into the woods and pause, ears raised. In the distance, more dogs bark and then suddenly stop. Only the wind and the noise of the pickup can be heard as John steers down another brush-covered street.

What do you got, Mr. John?

We got some grapefruit, Bo. Want some?

Yes, sir.

Alright. They're fresh.

You got oranges too?

Yes, sir. How are y'all doing today?

Hanging in there. Enjoying this weather.

Straight up. Not too hot to play some dominoes outside.

No, sir.

More young men run to the pickup, Hey, Mr. John! They put their hands behind their backs concealing, he assumes, drugs or perhaps even a weapon. John knows what they do. They rarely speak about it and he does not ask. There is the church and there is the street. He does not underestimate how quickly his interactions in the Donut Shop can go off the rails. Christians say, God will protect you. Yeah, John agrees, and wisdom too. Step back Rambo and think. The brain that God gave him provides wisdom. Wisdom has taught him to linger in the Donut Shop only long enough to maintain neighborhood connections and no longer.

Keeping it real, he reminds himself.

4

After handing out the fruit, John drops Jamez off at his grand-momma's apartment, where he looks forward to celebrating his birthday with her or one of his aunties. When he was little, they would take him to Chuck E. Cheese. Now he prefers McDonald's. He especially likes Big Macs. However, he enjoys Chick-fil-A, too, and might go there.

Jamez, his grandmomma, and Mayo once lived on Hale Drive, and he often heard gunshots. If the shots sounded close, he would run into the house. If not, he didn't worry about it. He has seen people firing guns on New Year's Eve but never at people. He remembers two guys with ski masks looking for a dude but they didn't find him so they shot up a tree instead.

Jamez has lost family. His grandmomma's son, Uncle Mayo, was shot. His great-great-grandmomma, an aunt, and a baby cousin also died. The baby drank lighter fluid. Jamez doesn't know how the aunt died. His great-great-grandmomma just stopped breathing one day but she was old. Things are cool, and then the next thing he knows someone's gone. Jamez knows a lot of people who have passed. It makes him feel odd and old.

Mayo took him to a lot of places. He'd be jamming his music in the car. He was always having a good time, and Jamez loved seeing him.

When Mayo died, his mother called him. Your uncle's been shot at your grandmomma's house, she said. Jamez started running. When he reached Hale Drive he saw everyone crying and then he began weeping. Blood pooled under Mayo's body. Bodine lived down the street and Jamez saw him apply CPR, but blood just shot out of Mayo. The family had an open casket funeral. When Jamez touched the body it felt hard and not like Mayo. Everything about him was gone.

5

John returns to the Village and leaves Da'Cino at the Lighthouse. Da'Cino walks up the porch steps, opens the door, steps inside. Sometimes he hesitates, as he worries he might break something just by looking at it. The house feels new, carries the aromas of fresh paint and plastic coverings instead of the stench of mold and mildew that filled the houses he grew up in. Da'Cino admires the kitchen. Wooden stools line up on one side of the counter, the walls bright white. Vinyl plank flooring catches the light. Two gray couches and two light brown leather chairs and a blue gray rug take up the living room; a white fireplace with a basket of firewood fills a corner. Two bedrooms complete with dressers and chests of drawers. Da'Cino considers the king-size bed in his room. He had never slept in anything so large. He could roll for days in that bed and not reach the other side, he thinks, laughing. It's as if suburban living has been brought to the 'hood, but the suburbs don't have gunshots. The absence of gunshots unnerves him when he leaves the Village. Like when a radiator shuts off, the abrupt silence consumes everything. Man, he thinks, this is too quiet for me. When he stops at a store, he takes note of every exit in case someone starts shooting. He lies awake at night thinking of things he's seen. In the Village, his mind is on speed dial, never pausing long on any one thought. The constant bombardment, the abrupt start and stop of it, the lack of predictability, allow no time for thought. He doesn't dwell on the bad stuff until he leaves. He can't relax until he returns to the Village.

Because so many of his homeboys have died, sometimes he forgets who's alive and who's dead. Kind of scary to get close to people because he doesn't know if they'll be shot. Scared for himself too. He understands death more than he understands life. Everybody shoots without a particular target. They just fire their weapons. If a homeboy asks him for a ride, he wonders, Does he have a beef with someone who might see us and start shooting? Bigg Man's good for that. He rides around with a whole bunch of people, and he doen't care who might be mad. But everyone likes him. He's flashy but he gives back. Everyone knows Bigg Man.

Sometimes old hurts surface in Da'Cino's memory and he relives pains he thought he had forgotten. He writes about them on his phone in a stream-of-consciousness tirade: *I grew up in the worst of hoods in the state of Prichard, Alabama. Most people know it as, don't go there! or think that the hood is nothing but drugs and black people and if you go in there you are going to get robbed. But I don't know it as that. I know it as my home! My life experience teacher! But most people outside the hood never think about the fact that everyone in the world is not like they think they are. If you don't believe me, let me tell you a story about a boy who was shy, didn't trust nobody and didn't have the best of living conditions. Let's get to the story now that I have your attention. A little boy grew up with 4 sisters and 2 other brothers and his mother and stepdad in a four bedroom house and they moved a lot so he always knew not to get comfortable because he knew in like a year they will move and he would have to start over with school and meeting friends. The stepdad was the meanest man the little boy had ever seen. The guy didn't care what he said or did to anyone. The momma sat there like it was OK. Matter of fact, she really never said anything or even left the house. The only time she ever talked was when she was drinking. The little boy would think she would really drink to stop the pain. She seemed unconnected from her kids and the world and this man running her life like she was just sitting back for the ride. The little boy started wetting the bed. You would think that this momma would want to know why her son is just wetting the bed. They beat him and sat him outside like he was a dog that they didn't want and he would sit outside in the cold for hours with his tee Shirt and boxers on! By being outside you would think this little boy would give up and turn his back on everyone well you would be right cause now this little boy's heart was hard and he didn't like no one who showed him love he pushed them away because love's nothing and ain't no one in this world alive he would allow to make him feel again it hurt too much no one can help him it was too late. He was no longer a part of their world and they weren't a part of his why should he care about people's feelings no one ever give a care about his!*

His birth father wanted nothing to do with Da'Cino and his siblings. He was six years old when he overheard him say, They ain't my kids. Years later, Da'Cino received a text from him on April 15: *Happy birthday, son.* He didn't reply. Da'Cino was born on March 15. Mr. John is more of a father to him.

As children, Da'Cino and his brothers didn't have friends. They were allowed to play outside only when they gave their stepdad, Joe, money to buy drugs. He wasn't a stepdad through marriage but through his sixteen-year relationship with Da'Cino's momma. He ran the house and stole from the children. He would hit the kids for not cleaning their room, for leaving the TV on, for coming home late from school. Da'Cino's momma never said anything. She'd cuss at them too, but she never raised a hand. She left that to Joe. He was good at smacking the shit out of them.

When he needed money, Joe could be nice. Da'Cino would give him two, three dollars and Joe would say, I can make it work with that, and he'd let Da'Cino go outside while he bought crack. Da'Cino joined the football team in middle school to escape the house. He didn't tell his momma and Joe when the season ended. I'll be at football practice, he would say so he could return home as late as possible. They never watched him play, so they didn't know he lied.

When Da'Cino graduated the fifth grade, Joe and his momma told him to quit school and work at Cozy Brown, a Prichard restaurant on US Highway 45. Joe knew the owner. Da'Cino was ten but tall, and the owner assumed he was of age and hired him full-time. For two months, Joe would stand in the back of the kitchen and tell Da'Cino to prepare collard greens, cut onions, and prep the grill. The owner paid Joe, Da'Cino didn't see a penny. Da'Cino's older brother, Jamichael, told one of his teachers about it and she notified the police. Summoned to court, Mary Dees and Joe were told by a judge they would be charged with child neglect if Da'Cino didn't return to school.

At home, Da'Cino's momma remained a passive presence except for three demands she made of her children: Before they left the house for school they had to recite the Twenty-third Psalm, their Social Security number, and her phone number or get a whooping from Joe. A teacher noticed bruises on their faces from the whoopings, so Joe started using a wooden paddle on their butts instead, striking them half a dozen times when they made a mistake. He swung that paddle hard enough to hit a home run. To this day, Da'Cino can rattle off the Twenty-third Psalm as fast as an auctioneer. The lord is my shepherd, I shall not want. Every morning, seven days a week. He never knew why that one psalm was so important to his momma. His social security number, too, what was up with that? But he memorized them both and her phone number to avoid being whooped.

As a boy, Da'Cino thought Jesus had superpowers because he could walk on water. He wanted to do that but without attending church. He didn't think much of the services. One pastor expected parishioners to talk in tongues. Da'Cino tried but couldn't fake it. All that jumping and running around shouting gibberish. Those people don't need to be in church, they're sick, he thought. That's not the Holy Spirit, that's the drugs from last night. What's wrong with these people? But his momma always made him go. He hated it. Hooping and hollering. Gave him nightmares.

The emphasis on church did not prevent Joe from recruiting Da'Cino and his brothers to shoplift. He could walk into a store and leave minutes later with a slab of ribs stuffed down his pants without so much as raising an eyebrow. He was that good. Da'Cino, Jamichael, and their younger brother, Marco, would follow him to a supermarket. Da'Cino would wear a baggy, button-down shirt with short sleeves. One afternoon he snatched a cupcake and put it in his breast pocket. The cashier saw him and said, Don't take that. Joe struck Da'Cino across the head, Boy, you know you ain't supposed to be stealing. Played it off like he was upset. Da'Cino couldn't say, Damn, but you told us to steal. His brothers never got caught.

Da'Cino doesn't know how Joe and his momma met. Probably at a hit house. Maybe he stole her heart, because he sure knew how to snatch everything else. He smelled cash. As a boy, Da'Cino hid what little money he earned cutting grass by stuffing it in a crack in the attic wall but Joe would always find it, no matter how obscure the hiding place. Da'Cino began wearing two pairs of pants and kept money in the pockets of the inside pair. When he went to bed, he assumed Joe would only search the pockets of the outside pair, but in the morning Da'Cino would discover that he had rifled through both pairs of pants and the rest of his clothes to take what few dollars he had tucked away.

In high school, Da'Cino and Jamichael decided to kill him. They would wait until he passed out one night, and then they would smash his head with a twenty-five-pound dumbbell. They went to the church to tell Mr. John about their plan. Da'Cino let Jamichael do the talking. We've decided to kill Joe, Jamichael told Mr. John. He's not going to mess with us no more. You really got to think about this, Mr. John said. We have, Jamichael replied. This could really scar your lives, Mr. John continued. The consequences will follow you. And what if you don't do it right and he lives? He won't be happy with the two of you. You think he's bad now. He'd be a whole lot worse. It's not worth it. You're getting ready to graduate high school in two years, Jamichael. You just started, Da'Cino. Think about that.

They mulled it over. After some consideration they agreed to hold off and allow Joe to live a little longer. It wasn't hard to dissuade them. Probably why they mentioned it to Mr. John in the first place. They didn't want to kill Joe, for real, but they were angry and didn't know what to do since their momma sure wouldn't do anything. But they had thought it through, rehearsed killing him in their minds, and been prepared to make it happen. Mr. John, Da'Cino thought, took them seriously. It was a good thing they had talked to him. It would've been a mess for sure: killing Joe with a dumbbell, cleaning up all the blood, and hiding his body. Just thinking about it made Da'Cino feel sick. A short time later, Joe moved to Michigan, where he had family. He didn't say goodbye, just left. Da'Cino and Jamichael didn't need a goodbye. They'd been prepared to kill him.

After Joe left, Da'Cino's momma took up with a dude named "Fish," whom she brought home one night. Da'Cino met him after school the next day and wondered, who is this man in our house? His sisters and brothers were equally curious. That's Fish, their momma told them. I met him at a hit house. She always enjoyed going out. But then she was diagnosed with diabetes and lost her left leg. She taught herself to walk with a prosthetic limb and continued drinking at hit houses until she fell. Fresh out of the hospital too. Still had stitches in her stump. Busted it wide open. After that she quit the hit houses but didn't stop drinking. Fish met her when she had two good legs.

Of all his momma's boyfriends, Da'Cino liked him the best. He could chill with Fish. He was slim and shaved his head and he had a herky-jerky way of walking like a puppeteer was yanking his strings. He talked fast, too fast. If words were cars, Fish would break speed records. He played video games with Da'Cino and helped around the house. He was more like a homeboy than a stepdad. He fathered Da'Cino's youngest brother, Keon, and he was always good about getting him up for school.

Da'Cino's momma and Fish are no longer together. She sees someone else. Fish still comes around when the new boyfriend has left the house and he has no place to stay. He drinks with Da'Cino's momma, but Da'Cino has never seen him with a hangover. He can just wake up and continue putting it down. He stays with Da'Cino's momma until she gets drunk and kicks him out. When she drinks, she gets bossy. You need to do this and this, she'll say. But when she's not drinking she doesn't speak. Da'Cino supposes his momma doesn't like sharing her beer with Fish. Too much of it anyway. But she must share it with her new boyfriend, so maybe it's something else about Fish that bothers her. He twists his brain into knots trying to understand her.

Da'Cino asked her for custody of Keon and Al. Al moved in with her after his momma, Da'Cino's sister Shameka, died of a heart attack in 2020. Thirty-two years old. Fell on the floor in her kitchen. Da'Cino tries not to think about it. Here he is worrying about gunshots, and a heart attack takes his sister. That's crazy.

Fish had no problem with Da'Cino taking the boys, but his momma wouldn't let him. She wanted the money to claim him at tax time. You can have the money, Da'Cino told her. I don't want it, just Keon. She still said no. He sees Keon at least once a week to offer the support and guidance he never received as a child. He tries not to stay too long or his mother will hit him up for money.

He doesn't doubt his momma loves Keon and Al in her way, but they need more than what she can offer. She never got on Da'Cino about things she should have when he was their age. Like not doing his homework and skipping classes. Da'Cino wishes she had because then he might not have dropped out of high school in the tenth grade. Maybe she didn't have the energy. Maybe she was depressed. She gets that way sometimes. She stopped taking her diabetes medicine a few months ago when her boyfriend was out of town. Fish found her passed out on her bed. He called Da'Cino: Your momma hasn't been eating, he said, and now she ain't waking up. Da'Cino asked: Have y'all got her nothing to eat? Have you been cooking for her? Fish said: She just hasn't been eating. Da'Cino thought maybe she wasn't hungry but Fish told him, No, she hasn't been eating for days. Da'Cino drove her to a hospital. A doctor told him she needed to stop drinking to revive her appetite and for the diabetes medicine to work. She followed his advice for a minute but after a week started drinking again. These days she drinks what she calls organic beers. She especially likes Michelob Ultra Pure Gold. She prefers it to other beers and doesn't think it has enough alcohol to hurt her. Da'Cino doesn't know about that. He doesn't know anything about organic beers. He thinks she's as OK as she is going to be. At fifty she has lived this way a long time.

Da'Cino thinks sometimes children need their parents to give them a shove. Getting beat by his stepdad, told he was nothing, and his momma sitting there letting him be treated like nothing made him think he was nothing. Da'Cino assumes she didn't know how to raise kids because she lost her parents at a young age. She probably wanted them to love her the way he wanted her to love him, but they were gone so she made the best of it living on her own with relatives. She had her first child at fifteen. She moved in with her older sister and just winged being a momma.

Da'Cino always felt like a stranger in her house. If it weren't for Keon, he wonders if he'd ever see her. She and Keon live in Chickasaw, only five minutes from the Village. Keon needs him, but he needs his momma too. Da'Cino doesn't. Not now. She messed up on him needing her when he needed her most. It's too late now. He's grown. She's still his momma, but that's about it.

6

At dusk, a church floodlight snaps on, trapping surprised bugs in its yellow glare. Beyond the beam, the Village settles into night. No porch lights to ward off the dark. Empty houses abandoned in the gloom. One or two people wander Baldwin Drive—phantom figures moving through the murk of a ghost town. Dogs bark from far away. The old people say voices cry out from graves now lost to woods. Seventy-two-year-old Julia Gordon on Lee Street off Dunlap Circle near the Donut Shop grew up with their stories. She emerges onto the sunken porch of her yellow house, moves with a decided limp from knee surgery, and like some weathered figurine settles in a cracked plastic chair in a corner. Peeled paint like dandruff at her feet. A rusted car squats in her yard. She stares at its lumpy shape. Gnats and mosquitoes dance above the tall grass and wild-flowers that compete for space with trash. She has no idea who once owned that vehicle. Its fossilized remains have some connection to a life she no longer recalls. A man ties his dog to it and pays her ten dollars a day to leave him there. He comes by to feed and water it—a strange arrangement she doesn't understand, but she takes his money. The dog whimpers, tears at the back seat. A faded, patterned dress shrouds Miz Julia's shrunken body, the thin cloth reeking of cigarettes and her own funk. Don't mess with Miz Julia, she says, as if she was not herself but someone observing her. Her smoker's voice claws up from the hollows of her throat, a volley of hoarse words that spill forth in a strained, constricted whisper. Her malevolent gaze focuses on an invisible audience.

Shut up, she says to the dog.

A barefoot man with dreadlocks emerges behind her.

You got milk? she asks him. I love milk. Miz Julia's a milk freak.

He ignores her, lights a smoke. She lets him live here but doesn't know his name or anything about him nor does she care to. She allows too many people to stay with her. Her house has become a crash pad for crackheads and drunks. They stink so bad she can't stand it, but she can't make them bathe. She settles for cigarettes, milk, and whatever else they might offer her. They take up her two bedrooms. She sleeps on her couch so she can look out the living room window to see who's coming. She woke up one morning four weeks ago to a man hitting her in the chest. Said she had something that belonged to him. She had not seen him or heard him. Talking about how she had taken his money. He hasn't been around lately. Miz Dolores told her to consider moving because of the people staying with her. Said she'd help her find an apartment but Miz Julia thinks she'd be a fool to pay rent when she owns a house. That would require most of her Social Security check. She worked hard for her house and doesn't want to leave it, but some part of her understands she probably should. She knows she has lost control of it. Strangers have taken over, but she can't rouse herself to act. She has settled into lethargy, endlessly complaining about freeloaders to anyone who will listen. People, she says, are something else. She huddles in her living room and retreats into a disjointed collage of memories and the distractions provided by an old black-and-white TV. The television is her friend. It keeps her company. She used to watch soap operas, movies. She loves Westerns, especially *Gunsmoke*. Every day at noon. She can't get enough of it, and *The Virginian* too. She'll be glad when this man in her house leaves. He walks up and down the street looking for dope. She doesn't get involved. She watches TV and waits for Matt Dillon to get the bad guys.

Sometimes she loses power because she has fallen behind on her bills. She feels truly alone then, the TV of no use to her. She stares at it, her reflection on the screen a mirror to her decrepit isolation. She has power now but it's still messed up. Every time workmen climb up those electric power poles to install cameras to stop people from dumping trash and dealing drugs in the Village, her outlets stop working for minutes at a time, but the dumping and dealing do not. Police ride around and look at young men with guns selling dope and throw their hands up.

Miz Julia is the kindest person in the world and don't nobody give her a dollar, she says to the man behind her. He doesn't respond.

You have a daddy?

I did, he tells her.

I loved my daddy.

The man retreats inside.

An older guy, Miz Julia's daddy, a Choctaw Indian from the Mississippi Delta somewhere up in the hills. He never cut his hair but he shaved every morning. He didn't talk much.

He worked as a longshoreman, Local 1410. He didn't drink or do any of that. His face had more lines than a tree has roots. He met her momma up at a Greyhound bus station in farm country north of Prichard. She told him her daddy beat her with a whip and she had run away. He took her in to help her out, and by him not knowing anybody else in the area, a woman that is, he stuck with her and that's how Miz Julia came into the world. They moved to Prichard. Miz Julia's momma had people here. The Village used to be a beautiful place. A nice-looking neighborhood. The green lawns shone. People moved out and trees started growing through the floors. Miz Julia's daddy used to bounce her on his knee. Was on his knee when police came to ask him about a dead man. Man deader than a doorknob. He had called her daddy a nigger. Her daddy steadily bouncing her like he didn't do nothing as the police asked their questions. They didn't lock him up. It was between her daddy and the dead man and none of their concern. The dead man wasn't talking and neither was her daddy.

Her momma played on her daddy when he was away working. She sent one of her men to school to give Miz Julia lunch money one afternoon. Mister, the school principal said, you awful light and she's awful black. You sure you're her daddy? Miz Julia laughs, a rumble in her throat. Her momma was something else. She had men outside the house waiting to be let inside.

As a child, Miz Julia didn't obey nobody. When she was twelve years old she worked as a babysitter and gave her momma the money. One day she didn't give her a cent and instead bought a phonograph with two 45 rpm records. Her momma made her take it all back. She and her momma never did get along. She always told Miz Julia that she wouldn't see twenty. Well, momma look at me now. God blessed me with fifty-three more years.

Her momma had another child, a son ten years younger than Miz Julia, and she loved him over her something fierce. She told Miz Julia, You're my child but I don't know where you come from. She married Miz Julia off to a man up-country. Fourteen or fifteen she was. She didn't like him and refused to lie with him. A woman killed him in her bathroom with a knife. Miz Julia doesn't know why. She wasn't one of those women who followed him around to see if he was cheating. He was going to do what he wanted to do anyway. She attended his funeral but she had no feelings for him.

Miz Julia takes after her daddy. He was a sharecropper in Mississippi when he was young and killed his boss man. Every time that motherfucker passed him he hit her daddy with his whip. Her daddy could only take so much. That boss man coming through there on his white pony all high and mighty. He slapped him around all day with that damn whip. Her daddy told the man next to him, That son of a bitch rides through here again, I'm going to take my sickle and knock him off his horse. Sometimes old people be sitting around telling lies but they also be telling the real truth, and Miz Julia's daddy told the truth. He whacked the boss man with his sickle just like he said he would and killed him. Miz Julia would have done the same.

She spent a good bit of her childhood in detention homes. The homes had cells like a prison. A Miz Pollock who worked on the weekends beat Miz Julia. There was a Miz Easton too. She directed the education department. Nice woman. She told Miz Julia's momma that she was a good student but her momma didn't believe her.

Miz Julia can no longer remember the name of the home. It was in the town right up the road from Prichard. No, not Mobile. Where the bus goes down and turns. Not at Spring-Hill Avenue but the other one going across town. You go down there to the Prichard bus station and you catch a bus, number 45. Take you right there if you visiting. The police will take you if you're staying.

Miz Julia laughs her coarse laugh.

She has lived all over. A radio station, WOMZ, advertised jobs for young Black women up north. The job provided room and board. Didn't have to worry about nothing. Miz Julia was but fifteen back living with her momma and daddy after her husband died. She ran away, took a bus to New York for a housekeeping job in Long Island. When she arrived and saw all the bright lights of Manhattan she said to herself, Hello. She'll never forget that. So bright at night. The city looked like a big garbage can in the morning. Trash everywhere. She caught a train to Westbury, Long Island. Pretty as pretty can be. Green. Homes like gingerbread houses. She cleaned the house of a Dr. George Arnold and stayed in a little apartment in the back. Miz Julia would sneak a couple of drinks when she was alone. The family kept a whole bar. She'd have a smoke and then pour herself a glassful of whiskey and another glassful of ice water. She cooked dinner for the Arnolds and ate what they did not, wrapping it in newspaper for something to snack on at night. She worked for two weeks before her momma found out where she was and called her home.

She left home again in 1966 at sixteen. Her momma had died of cancer and her daddy didn't need her. He was always off working, so she rode up to Detroit with her Aunt Salina, who had family there. Took a minute driving to Michigan. Cloudy all the time in Detroit. She wondered, Do it ever sunshine up here? But she ended up liking Michigan. Winters were pretty cold. She never did get used to walking in all that snow. Different from Alabama. She saw things in Detroit she had only seen on TV. People walking around in mink coats, driving Cadillacs and stuff. New York was like that too.

Miz Julia remained in Detroit and worked as a housekeeper until 1998, when her daddy called. He was sick and had no one to look after him. You need to come home, he told her. She cared for him and when she wasn't with him she worked, housekeeping mostly. One boss lady told her, You're a maid from hell, because she wouldn't take no shit. You think you're crazy, Miz Julia will show you crazy, she told her. Maybe she was afraid of Miz Julia because she kept her on. She cleaned and cooked and watched *The Young and the Restless* at eleven o'clock. Baked cakes every week, and fruit pies.

After work, she'd go out and play blackjack and dance at a hit house owned by a man named Charles on Baldwin Drive. Still there. His white head of hair tucked up under a straw hat. He would knock on her window at two in the morning after he closed. Get up, Julia, let's ride. He had a lot of cars. Took her up on Highway 45. She smoked weed back then. Marijuana made her laugh. They'd stop at Burger King, and Charles would put his arm around her. You gay, Julia? he asked her one night when she didn't respond to his advances. No, she said, I just don't want you.

She met Mr. John and Miz Dolores a short time after they came to the Village. She thought they had moved in to the old crack house. No, they explained, they had turned it into a church. Damn, Miz Julia said. She maintained a vegetable garden for them. Had little bitty tomatoes. Collard greens, turnips, potatoes too. Kids would smash the tomatoes. After a while, Miz Julia grew discouraged or tired—she doesn't know which—and the vegetable garden turned to weeds, although collard greens still grow in that tiny patch of ground she tended.

As a child, she recalls Alabama Village as a place Black people didn't go unless they were domestic workers. White families lived here then. White folks would let their dogs out to chase Black kids cutting through the Village to get home after school. When the dogs got to Whistler Street on the outer edges of the Village, they'd turn around and go home. Their territory stopped there. If the kids made it to Whistler, they were good and they'd throw rocks at the dogs. Prichard had a zoo in those days on Wilson Avenue. Black people couldn't go to it. They went to the zoo in New Orleans.

Prichard elected its first Black mayor, Algernon Johnson Cooper, in 1972. Until then, Black people had little influence on the city's politics. Prichard was a growing city then and it had money. Mobile was twice as big but Prichard was hopping and Alabama Village a quiet place to live. If anyone could see how it was back in 1972 compared to now, they wouldn't believe it was the same place. Desegregation, white flight, families started moving out. The Village became a place where no one wanted to live but poor people. So many shootings and cuttings. Once it started going down, there was nobody to help pick it back up. Most people wouldn't ride through now.

There was this lady, a nurse Miz Julia knew. One time she was trying to find Hale Drive and the street signs were down so she asked some guys on a street corner, Where's Hale Drive? and they said this whole area is hell. She had to spell the name before they understood. She helped disabled patients both Black and white. One white man told her, You're the kind of

woman I would have loved to have as a wife. You know I'm
Black, she said. Oh, I don't care, he said. Next door to him
was a white lady who lived with her husband and son. She was
seventy-two, couldn't walk but was very nice. Liked to sit in her
living room and watch soap operas and talk about the different
characters. Kept up to date on each one. She had worked at
one time. Not a professional job. A laborer. Her son was on the
special side. Husband did odd jobs.

Can't even see street signs now because of all the trees. Miz
Julia can't believe how the Village has turned. She figures like
everything else, like life itself, the Village has just run its course.

Most nights, the shooting around her house begins at about
ten o'clock. Blasts of gunfire and then a thudding *whump,
whump* shakes the air. The heaviness of the noise. It explodes
around Miz Julia's property rattling the walls followed by the
pop, pop, pop of semiautomatic gunfire. The shooter probably
has a problem with another guy. When they see each other they
start going at it. Most likely they know where each other hangs
out. It's been like this for weeks, months, years.

The wind presses against Miz Julia's house and the old boards
groan. Moonlight carves the road. The man staying with her
leaves without a glance. She watches him walk toward Dunlap.
Not one dollar from him, she mutters. Nothing for cigarettes
or milk. Her daddy, he was the kindest man. She would drive
him all around. He was eighty-some years old when he died in
2000. Her heart doesn't ache for no man but him. He was all
she ever had.

7

Morning. Strings of misty air like strands of cotton. The faint noise of dogs barking. A fox pokes its head out from beneath bushes outside a crumbling house before it retreats. A young woman follows the cut from Gulf Village into Alabama Village. She tugs at a thin jacket too big for her body, rubs her bare legs, and shambles forward. She crosses Baldwin, walks behind the church to Dunlap, and looks up and down the street with an uncomprehending stare. Head bowed, she meanders across Miz Julia's yard, knee-high grass slapping at her legs, a chaos of bugs roused, and she moves unhindered by their aggravation, waving her arms with little conviction.

Old men sit in a field near the Donut Shop in folding chairs beneath a tree, bottled beers at their feet. The ground around them strewn with trash. Plastic grocery bags snagged on thorny shrubs snap in the wind. Houses slanting into their foundations shine dew-waxed in the emerging light. A rack of thin clouds trawls across an otherwise empty sky edged with pink light. The men slow-sip their beers, talk.

I told Trevor, Trevor be thinking I'm lying, but I told him there was this lady on Dunlap and she come to her door in the morning time and step out on her porch and she throwed her slop out onto the grass and they was rabbits right out there eating that slop. Man, I thought they was vegetarians. But those motherfuckers was eating that slop. Meat-eating rabbits, I'm talking about.

Rabbits was?

If they wasn't eating that slop, they was eating the grass around it which is the same thing 'cause the slop be in the grass like gravy.

No wonder they so big.

They fat too.

That's what I'm saying, they big.

Greasy slop mixed with that water and she threw it over there and they ate it.

She going to have a lot of dogs by doing that.

Cats too. Five or six of them come out around here. All of them black cats too.

She'll have her share of bad luck or I'm lying.

Cats could be in for some trouble with meat eating rabbits.

Twenty-eight-year-old Barry Alton rides past the men on his bicycle. Red hair, bright as fire, freckled face. He has a temp job on Highway 90 in Mobile behind a Greyhound bus station. Power washing an apartment building. Tomorrow he'll operate a forklift in Pensacola. He likes his coffee, thinks his coworkers will ban him from the coffeepot at work, he drinks that much.

Stayed in the Village all his life in the same house he grew up in as a child. He lives with a friend who he hopes gets gone sooner rather than later. Known him for three years but he ain't paying for nothing. Barry, he says, I'll get it to you. But he never does. He ain't stole nothing yet, a good thing. Everybody else steals from him but so far his friend hasn't. Give him time.

No one in Barry's family lives in the Village—or in Prichard for that matter. His momma and daddy split up when he was eleven, thirteen, he forgets which. She went back to her parents or whatever. He stayed with his daddy until the old man moved to Mississippi or somewhere like that. The sky turns blue, the dappled light pooling around him as he rides. Blue jays jeer and squirrels scamper beside the road, then flee as Barry rides past. The wheels disturb pebbles, the noise of him moving over them, a patchwork of scratches on the smooth air, Dunlap Circle empty but for his leaving and the raucous laughter of the men.

8

Bigg Man cruises past Miz Julia's house and turns onto Barbour Drive and then onto Baldwin and stops at the church. He takes comfort here, sitting alone when no one is about. He has never told Mr. John and Miz Dolores that he likes coming here by himself. He's not ashamed, just something he does and it's no one's business but his own. He believes in God. Mr. John baptized him. Bigg Man considers himself a good person, not a perfect person but a good one, friendly and kindhearted, but he won't let nobody disrespect him. He has a bad temper, he knows, but thinks he has it under control. He loves Mr. John and Miz Dolores. They help anyone. He has never seen any two people give of themselves like they do. They pay bills, provide food, furnish clothes, and talk about Jesus like he's this cool dude who lives down the block. They do more than they should, way more. Bigg Man will let no harm come to them.

Rain begins falling and he turns on the windshield wipers and blasts the defrost, dials it down when it gets too hot. He and his cousin Lawrence were at Miz Phyllis's house on the front porch when they first saw Mr. John and Miz Dolores in a small blue pickup. Bigg Man and Lawrence were about ten or nine. Mr. John and Miz Dolores passed them and then came around again to check things out. The Village was a poor, all-Black neighborhood. It wasn't common to see two white people. Bigg Man and Lawrence thought, Police. They hesitated before they got up the nerve to approach them. Why're y'all here? Bold boys. This was their neighborhood. You know, you shouldn't be over here. First thing out of Mr. John's mouth: He wanted to establish a ministry. It would include Bible study and after-school programs. Bigg Man and Lawrence knew who God was. Other church organizations had come to the Village. Word of Life Church had a purple bus, and the Destination Church Dream Center had a yellow one. Volunteer drivers would pick up families for church services, but then they stopped. No church stuck around the Village for long. Too much shooting and not much repentance. Bigg Man and Lawrence figured Mr. John and Miz Dolores would quit on them too. Especially being white. They would be tore up.

Miz Dolores always calls him Corey—her and his girlfriends—but Mr. John and everyone else calls him Bigg Man. He has had that name as far back as he can remember. He can't say why but he owns it now. He weighed a few pounds more than he should have as a boy and he supposes his family just decided to call him Bigg Man. He doesn't mind women calling him Corey. At twenty-five he has had a few girlfriends. He's fathered four children, including Corey Jr., whose photo he put on the Memorial Wall.

Corey Jr. had been with his momma, Dynesha Harris, and her boyfriend, Tony Fowler, the night he died on January 31, 2020, at the Red Roof Inn in Mobile near Dauphin Street. Dynesha called Bigg Man and told him to come to the hospital. He assumed Junior had fallen, broken a bone or something. When he reached the emergency room, Dynesha stared at him without moving or speaking. She looked small. The look in her eyes told him it was worse than he thought, much worse. Something deep had happened, something bad deep. Then she told him: Corey Jr. had shot himself in the back of his head while she was in the shower and Tony slept. Bigg Man went off, shouting and yelling and hitting walls. Two security officers held him. They told him Corey Jr. should be OK. Bigg Man thinks they just wanted to calm him, but they only added to his confusion. Even if Junior is OK, he thought, he won't be the same person. He was shot in the head. Something's going to be missing. Something won't be right. Alive or dead, Bigg Man will have lost his son.

He called Mr. John and they met at the ministry, prayed for guidance, and talked. That was comforting as far as it went, but Bigg Man needed something more. Counseling wasn't going to work. He stayed in his house for three months crying and smoking weed to ease his mind. Every time he thinks about Junior he breaks down and gets high to put him out of his mind. He gets loaded, for real. Not to do anything crazy but to avoid thinking about Junior, to avoid everything but crying. Some people can't take their baby dying. He tries to be strong. To stay strong he gets high. Tony is in jail for drugs. When he gets out there's no telling what Bigg Man will do. One thing's for sure: He'll want him to explain how a two-year-old lifted a pistol and shot himself in the back of his head.

Bigg Man has spent his entire life in the Village. His daddy rotated in and out of prison. He had two mothers, his real momma and Auntie Phyllis, who treated him like her own son. When he needed them, they took care of him. His daddy did his part when he was out of prison. Bigg Man hears from him from time to time but he doesn't need him. Not now. He's grown. A child needs his daddy, not a man.

He remembers how he and Lawrence helped Mr. John and Miz Dolores pick up trash on Baldwin, and how they would give them lunch, but once he reached his teens he didn't think they could do much more for him. No one, not even Mr. John and Miz Dolores, can tell an adult how to behave. They help families meet their needs, but people will always have wants too. When he was a boy and he wanted something and Light of the Village didn't have it, he'd steal it. Now he has money and he can buy pretty much whatever he wants.

He counts on his fingers: At fourteen, he did a year in juvenile. Got out for three, four months and went back in for another year. Went back again when he was seventeen, got out at eighteen. Went in once more at twenty-three, got out at twenty-four. Most of it for selling marijuana. But he was never arrested for distribution, just possession.

Mr. John and Miz Dolores visited him in prison and Mr. John would ask him what he planned to do to be a better person when he got out, and Bigg Man always answered, I'm going to change. But he never did. He meant what he said, but once he hit the streets, his mind moved in an entirely different direction. What made sense in prison no longer applied.

He and another dude got into it about a girl one time. The girl told Bigg Man she was with him and then turned around and told the dude he was her man. The dude saw them together one day and thought Bigg Man was trying to backdoor him. He pulled out a gun and Bigg Man drew his Glock. Look, I'm going to put my gun down, Bigg Man told him. I ain't trying to go there with you about no girl. I didn't know you were talking to her. The dude put up his gun. You right, he told Bigg Man.

Sometimes Bigg Man wonders what would have happened if he had started shooting. Where would he be now? Where would the dude be? Would they even be alive?

Bigg Man likes to wash cars and work on construction projects with a friend he met in prison. He does other things to make money, fast money. The kind of money that buys new cars and clothes and fur coats. The people who know what he's talking about know, and the people who don't, don't. He ain't that fat little boy no more. He's still called Bigg Man but for a different reason now. Many days he feels like Old Bigg Man. The police watch him. He doesn't trust the people on the street who do business with him. He wants to buy an eighteen-wheeler and travel state to state delivering whatever. He talked to Miz Dolores about that not too long ago. Get his commercial driver's license. See a little of the country and leave the Village, but he can't conceive of living anywhere else. That holds him back. Probably why he hasn't followed up with Miz Dolores about studying for his CDL. How do you leave everything you know? He recently told Lawrence, You know what? I'm not always going to sell drugs. I do got a brain.

He wants off the fast money. If he invests in rigs, they'll bring him more money legally than what he's doing illegally. Fast money comes with envy. People want to rob him, set him up for prison. He told Lawrence not to tell Auntie Phyllis about his plans. She needs him to buy her a car. That'll require fast money. Then he'll stop, he swears. He'll talk to Miz Dolores again and get his CDL. Once he has it, he'll figure out how to leave the Village and everything he has known. Even leave Bigg Man and just go by Corey.

If he could return to his childhood, he'd graduate from high school, enroll in college, and be a nerd. But it's too late for that.

He doesn't think he'd fit in. He's smart but he doesn't believe he has the kind of intelligence necessary for school. He was never much on book learning. If he tried to remake himself now and flunked out, people would know and that would affect their opinion of him. He'd have to assert his pride and that would result in a shooting. He can avoid all that by not trying. However, if he could get an athletic scholarship, he'd sign up for college today. But he'd have to be a hella player for real. He was good once but not now, too fat. If a coach told him, You work out, you can play football, he would do it. Get your body back in shape and in six months we'll let you play sports, he'd be on it. But that won't happen. No coach or anybody else will say that to him. He is who he is: Bigg Man. That's how people know him. They look up to him. He's respected. Who would he be outside the Village?

His phone rings. Bigg Man picks up. Lawrence.

What up, cuz?

9

Lawrence talks to Bigg Man for a minute and then gets off the phone. Just checking in, see what's going on. They talk every day about nothing. They have that kind of bond. Hardly anyone calls Lawrence by his name. He's LRG, because just like Bigg Man he has some heft to him. But he doesn't have Bigg Man's reputation. He's LRG but not in the street sense.

Lawrence lives in Chickasaw. He delivers merchandise for Lowe's and Xerox Corporation in Mobile and will keep at it as long as it pays, and until something better comes along. He has an eight-year-old boy and keeps him away from the street. He can only do so much, however, before his child begins making his own choices. He wants to be a positive influence and instill in him the capacity to resist temptation. Lawrence won't take him to Light of the Village. They could be at the church ready to attend Bible study and someone starts shooting. It just takes only one bullet to kill a child and his father. Look what happened to little Corey.

Lawrence keeps focused on what's best for his son. He and the boy's momma split up but the child means everything to him. A lot of fathers don't stay in their children's lives. They cheat, and the mommas get angry and don't let them see their kids. Lawrence didn't cheat. His son's momma decided to leave him for her own reasons. As long as he can see him, she can do what she wants.

When Lawrence was a kid, people didn't kill first and do whatever later. Back then it was all about the hustle. Get a few dollars. The drug dealers wouldn't let kids see what they were doing. Of course, kids knew but it wasn't in their faces like it is now. They didn't conduct transactions in front of just anyone. If they saw Lawrence or any kid hanging around, they told them to go play. Now, no one cares what anyone sees.

Most people in the Village can't see themselves outside of it. They think they can't make it anywhere else. They feel stuck but people with strong minds can get out. If they can't resist temptation, that's on them. They can always help a friend but they don't have to get mixed up in their business, especially if that business is guns and drugs. They can help from a distance; they don't have to stay in the Village. He and Bigg Man are as close as brothers, but Lawrence keeps to his own lane. He ain't going to hang with him on the street.

Lawrence believes the man he is now is a result of being around Mr. John and Miz Dolores. As a kid, he'd ride with Mr. John in his pickup. They just clicked. Even now. If they pass each other on the interstate, Lawrence calls him on his cell phone. I seen you, Mr. John. I seen you too, Bo.

Bigg Man had a stronger relationship with Miz Dolores. He could get away with some things with her. He was her pet. Everything she told him to do he would do. Miz Dolores is strong. Look you straight in the eye and you'll be doing what she tell you, for real. Bigg Man never wanted to let her down.

Short little thing but when she looked at him with that big old smile, before Bigg Man knew it he was in another world. She would be steady talking and he would be steady doing what she was telling him to do. He didn't hear nothing but her. She'd say, Thank you, at the end of it. Don't let her hold your arm as she's talking to you. You're gone then. She got you.

Bigg Man wanted to get out on his own so he rented a house in the Village. He was already into that lifestyle so he had no problem living there. Lawrence never lived that life. He hung around older people and was influenced by their wisdom. He looked up to four older men: his daddy, his stepdaddy, an uncle who was just like a daddy, and a neighbor, Mr. Charles. He used to fix Lawrence's bicycle. Sometimes the devil uses money to trap you, Charles would warn him: If you don't have much, that's how he'll get you. Lawrence heeded his words. To this day, people tell him he has an old spirit. He thinks that's because he carries the words of the grown folk who influenced him.

Bigg Man hung with guys into that fast money. That's all he saw then and all he knows or wants to know now. He got into the drug game when he was fifteen or sixteen. Mr. John talked to him all the time but once that fast money pulled him in, wasn't nobody going to pull him out, not even Mr. John. Lawrence knows Bigg Man understands right from wrong but he rationalizes his lifestyle by helping people out. He's the type of person if he got it, you got it. If you can pay him back he'll accept it, but if you can't he'll work with you. He thinks that if he gives someone a hand and doesn't ask for anything in return, he can stay in the game longer because he won't have enemies. It doesn't really work like that, Lawrence has told him. The game is dangerous no matter how cool you are.

He knows how to work. He had one job with a day-labor

outfit and he worked with a construction crew on Cottage Hill Place in Mobile. He did that for a good little while, and worked at The Krystal in Saraland, a burger place, for six months. He's had at least three or four legitimate jobs. He gets tired of the street. Who wouldn't? He faces a lot of jealousy. Bigg Man's the type of dude who can go to prison today, stay in there for a year, get out and have as much money as a guy who had been hustling the entire year he was in prison. Lawrence doesn't know what it is. Bigg Man can just get it. People resent him. Some of them hate him, for real.

10

Dolores remembers when Bigg Man dropped by the ministry to ask about getting his commercial driver's license. She hadn't seen him for God knows how long. He grew up in the church. Oh, goodness, he could be a handful, but as he got older he dropped by less and less.

He had driven to the church on a cold January day while John was out on an errand. Bigg Man parked. He stepped out of his car, the tight braids of his hair hanging about his forehead. He left the engine running and the door open and approached Dolores, pausing to say hello to boys and girls in the ministry's after-school program. They chased each other shouting, reaching for him to pick them up. His white windbreaker and red plaid pants rippled from a brittle breeze. He smiled, diamond grillz on his teeth. He walked with his chest out as if he was pushing obstacles aside. He always had a presence.

A few years ago, as volunteers served lunch, two guys got into it at the church. Voices raised until one of them relented, got quiet, and raised his hands, Awright, awright, but the other dude, Bigg Man's younger brother, "Kirk-Kirk," felt no reason to relent. Bigg Man approached them.

We're at the church, y'all, he said in an even voice without getting loud. We're going to be gentlemen and this is not how we're going to handle our business. We never handle our business at the church. We're going to be respectful and if we can't do that we're going to have a problem outside of the church. Are we ready to calm down?

Dude with his hands up said, I'm cool. Kirk-Kirk remained angry but he agreed. Yeah, I'm cool. Bigg Man said, Good, let's eat.

Hey, Corey! Dolores shouted.

Bigg Man smiled, a thousand-watt smile that lit up his face. A hard layer of pretense peeled off of him. Dolores hugged him and he wrapped his arms around her, enveloping her body. When they released each other, Bigg Man told Dolores he wanted to drive trucks. Would she help him apply for a CDL?

Yes, she said. Whatever you need to do, let's do it.

He nodded OK, smiled at her enthusiasm. For no apparent reason he told her that when he hears of someone in need, he helps them with food and a hotel room. Dolores thought he wanted her to know he was doing good things even though he may not be involved in good things himself.

That's so sweet, she said. And you know, you're always welcome here.

He offered to take her and John to lunch. He would pay for it.

Anywhere you want, Bigg Man said.

Oh thank you, she said.

I mean it, Bigg Man said.

OK.

Wherever you want, he said again. Just tell me where and the day you want to go out.

John drove up, parked, and joined them.

What's up, Bo? he said.

Bigg Man smiled again. He told John what he had told Dolores: He wanted to take them to lunch. Are you going to eat the whole cake again? John asked. Oh, man, Bigg Man said and laughed, almost blushing.

When Bigg Man was ten, John and Dolores treated him, Da'Cino, and some other boys to a buffet at a Golden Corral restaurant in Mobile. They had never been to a restaurant let alone a buffet. Bigg Man took an entire chocolate cake and carried it back to their table. Dude, what are you doing? John said. Bigg Man could have cared less. He sat down and started eating the cake, the whole cake, his grin as wide as the table. We can't take you anywhere! Dolores said laughing.

She reminded him about the shoes he stole. Bigg Man was still a kid, but he had already become a thief. One week he wanted new shoes, a status thing. Dolores spoke to him about the importance of earning money to buy shoes. They talked and prayed about it. A few days later, he came to the church wearing new brown sneakers. She looked Bigg Man in the eye. She smiled but she wasn't laughing. I thought you didn't have any money, Dolores said in a soft voice but with a quiet intensity making it clear she expected him to tell her the truth.

Did you steal those shoes?

Bigg Man looked at the ground.

Yes.

And you're walking around in them?

Yes.

That's wrong, Corey.

Dolores gave him a choice. He could be suspended from the church or he could dig a hole and bury the shoes. He took them off and agreed to dig the hole. She made him dig a deep, deep hole so he couldn't unearth them later. A sunny day. The heat bore down on him as he dug, and he began to sweat. Other kids watched him. As he dug, Dolores told him the hole would serve as an example of what he was doing to his future. Look, by stealing you're digging a hole for your life, she said. You have to stop doing bad things. Bigg Man continued digging. He didn't complain. Dolores stood and watched him, hands on hips. The other children helped him. That's good enough, Dolores said after an hour. The hole looked as deep as a grave. Now put the shoes in. Bigg Man did. OK. Cover them up. Bigg Man began shoveling dirt on top of them. The children watching helped him fill it. The shoes are gone, Dolores said when they finished. This type of behavior is gone too. We're done with this. Bigg Man remained quiet, almost stoic, respectful. He didn't talk back, not once. He didn't say anything.

Bigg Man laughed at the memory. Pointing across the street, John and Dolores told him they bought the Twiley house, the only house still standing in the otherwise vacant lots around the church. We'll use it as a shelter for teenagers, Dolores said.

If you do that, Bigg Man said, you have to establish rules. Don't let them listen to rap music with bad words. No violent video games. No girls in the house. Bible study should be mandatory and held every day. Rules should be posted on the wall.

Dolores couldn't help but think that Bigg Man was never one to follow rules. But he was twenty-five now, no longer a child. He wanted to get his CDL. Perhaps he had grown weary of street life. Perhaps his emphasis on rules was his way of letting her and John know he understood he needed to change.

Da'Cino snapped a picture of him with John and Dolores before he left. In the photo, Bigg Man stands between them with his arms draped around their shoulders. He smiles but looks tired. John wears sunglasses and cocks his head toward Bigg Man. Dolores flashes a toothy grin.

Call me about lunch, he reminded them.

You're always welcome here, Dolores said again. You know that.

She watched him leave, wondering when or if she would see him again. Bigg Man always knew the direction he wanted to take with his life: anyplace that brought in money. Dolores had no idea Lawrence would be doing so well. As the children she has known grow older, she can usually tell if they're being drawn into the street life. She will ask after them and see them every so often until they disappear, but Lawrence surprised everyone. He became a truck driver and fathered a child. She has no idea if he attends a church but he has a foundation. He's being a dad. He's raising his son. Bigg Man was always about status. He craved things. She knew the rumors about his lifestyle. His money doesn't come from selling candy, and she worried where that would lead.

———

In many ways, Dolores has been training to do ministry work since she was a child. Her family lived across the street from their church in Las Cruces, New Mexico, and she went to Mass with her family every Sunday and attended all the holy days of obligation. Before she met John, Dolores had considered becoming a nun.

She hates the idea that people think of the Village as a place to avoid. To her the families here mean more than the crime that makes the news. A person can know good and still grapple with temptation, she believes. She sees the person behind the gun. They are friendly and funny. They struggle, grieve, and yet survive. It amazes her how they persevere and look out for one another.

Her memories of each child who has passed through the ministry fulfill her. She has laughed with them, held them, and cried with them. Dolores taught Bigg Man how to read. He could read a little but needed practice. He took to it. She'd listen to him read aloud and help him. He just needed tutoring. He had the ability. He was always very smart.

She and John encouraged two teenagers, Joseph Torres and Johiterio, Miz Betty's son, to follow their interest in writing. How about you write rap? they suggested. They started rapping at Sunday services and the after-school program, and even did a few songs at the University of Mobile at a fundraising event for the church. Street and Christian, they called themselves. Bigg Man tried to join but Joseph and Johiterio didn't want him because they didn't think he was very good, so he wrote his own songs. She remembers the lyrics to one of them: *Devil why / do you make me want to sin / Devil why?* Da'Cino would hype Street and Christian to his friends but he refused to rap or dance.

The boys would always act so tough. Even when they were little. Dolores and John took some Village kids to the beach one summer and the boys paraded around in their little life jackets like gunslingers but when they saw the waves surge onto the beach, they ran from them. Big, tall boys laughing and screaming and dancing as the water lapped their feet. Kids being kids. Those memories remain among her most precious. She can see each child as they were. Like Corey. Like Da'Cino. Like Mayo. Just before he died, Mayo saw Dolores arranging a tent for a church event. Miz Dolores, do you need help? Yes, I do, she answered. I'll help you, Mayo replied. They put up decorations and laughed and as they laughed, a boy came up and said another boy had brought a toy gun to the church, something John and Dolores didn't tolerate. Mayo said, I'll talk to him. He took the boy with the gun aside and in a little while the boy approached Dolores and apologized. A few weeks later, Mayo died.

11

In a hallway a short distance from where Dolores reflects on Mayo, twenty-eight-year-old Jesenda Brown cleans. A yellow bucket filled with soapy water stands in a corner. Bottles of disinfectant spray and rags take up a table. She washes the counters, then takes a packet of Lysol Lemon and Lime Blossom, and gets on her knees to clean the baseboards which take a lot of scrubbing because of all the scuffs. With that done she goes on to the sweeping and mopping. She feels good when everything shines. I did that, she thinks. She is especially pleased on days like this when she doesn't rush because then she has time to linger and take pride in her work. She brushes her long hair back from her shoulders, tugs at a T-shirt damp with sweat, and slaps her hands against her jeans to dry them.

Good morning, Miz Dolores, Jesenda says, when Dolores greets her. Not, Hi or Hey, but Good morning. And she doesn't refer to her by her nickname, "D.Lo." It's the professional thing to do, she believes, greeting her employer in a respectful, formal manner. For months the ministry has been a mainstay of Jesenda's startup, Jesenda's Cleaning Service. She recently established a business page on Facebook to attract customers. People have called, not many, but some. She has customers, none of them steady. Light of the Village is the only regular cleaning job she has. Everybody else can't make up their minds. They may ask her to clean one week but not the next. She needs consistency, the church job isn't enough.

She intends to post on Angie's List to attract more business. Then she thinks she will be super busy. She should get more serious about it because she really doesn't want to clean; she wants to get big enough to hire people to clean. She needs to use her time better. Use it to arrange contracts with schools and hospitals that would pay her big money. She wants a car to get around and hopes to buy one in a couple of weeks. Her year-end goal: to earn $2,400 a month. That would be good. That would be perfect. She should talk to Miz Dolores for job leads. She has to put more time into marketing, promotion. She recently bought a computer but needs to find a good internet service. Her head hurts thinking about it.

To earn that much a month she needs to stop spending so much time doing too much of nothing. Just not working. She wants to get away. Get away from Prichard, from Mobile. Far, far away. Miz Dolores tells her, Oh you can go to Saraland, but Jesenda wants to *move*. She wants to see places. So many things, where to start? Go to Michigan or Arizona or California. See other stuff.

She catalogs her faults. Making excuses, that's a big one. She has to focus on her business. Jesenda doesn't question her choice of a career. A cleaning business makes sense. She was always neat. Her life did not have much order as a child but she kept the spaces she occupied tidy. When she ran away from a foster home, she would connect with a boyfriend and clean his apartment. As an adult she thought, Why not use that skill to earn a living instead of working for other people? Her motto: Maintain stability through responsibility. A bumper-sticker slogan she repeats as though she sat through a self-empowerment seminar but she thought of it herself. She wants to own a home, not rent a subsidized house. Her children—a four-year-old son, Shane but whom she calls Prince, and two daughters, seven-year-old Taylor and five-year-old Londyne—should not have to struggle as she does now. If she provides them with stability, they can go to college and beyond. She wants them to become doctors and lawyers and make good money. She doesn't want them to feel stuck in one place. She hopes they pursue their dreams, follow their hearts, and never fear to try something new—but don't act like a fool at the same time. She has spoken to them about the loss of her momma and daddy. They know her momma died when she was young. Life was never the same. Not all bad but not the same. She tells them, One day, should God want to take me, I may not be here for you, and so she feels she must teach them what they need to know now. She had no idea what to do when she had her first period. Stuff like shouldn't be picked up any old kind of way. They're a little young but they should hear it from her.

She hopes her children will one day tell their friends, My momma is doing good. She wants them to brag about what she has accomplished and strive to do better. Londyne told her the other day, Momma, I want to have me a cleaning service like you when I grow up. No, Londyne, Jesenda said, running a cleaning service is good but if you get a cleaning service you don't want to be the one doing all the work like me. How am I going to get a cleaning service if I don't do no work, momma? You hire people to do the work. You got to go to school and learn about handling your money and numbers and stuff and you make your money and hire people. You carry it forward to where I haven't got. That's success.

Each of her children has a different father. That doesn't bother Jesenda. Many people, she understands, would disapprove. They will say what they will about her sleeping with different men and that's fine. She doesn't care what anyone thinks. It's her life, not theirs, and she loves her kids. No one can say otherwise. She married Taylor's daddy. Married about a year but they had been together for a minute before he proposed. He ain't nobody to know. No good. He cheated. Her daughters attend school and Prince stays in day care when she works. Most every adult Prince has known has passed, and he knows they ain't coming back. When people die she tells her children, That's something that just happens. Everyone dies one day. I'm gonna die; you're gonna die; we all gonna die. No, momma you ain't gonna die, they tell her, we're not gonna to die. She leaves it at that. She doesn't want them to think they'll all die right now. She never brings it up unless someone passes.

Jesenda wrings the mop, and sets it in a corner, and takes a sponge to wipe down walls. Sometimes Taylor or her fifteen-year-old nephew, Lavon, helps her. Lavon is with her today because he was suspended from school.

You sweep the bathroom?

Yeah, auntie, I just swept the bathroom.

Jesenda walks over and looks at it.

Now look at that tile, Lavon. Still dust on it.

God! I know how to clean up!

I didn't say you don't know how to clean up. You're just not focused.

I am focused.

You told me you'd help, Jesenda says. You said, I'll help you, auntie, and I said, OK. If you help me I'll pay you. But I'm not paying you for this now. I can do without that. Not even half good.

I'm focused.

You're a character. Just sit down.

Lavon stalks off. Family, Jesenda mutters. Hard to be with them, hard to be without them. Family is family, though. Over the weekend, she watched her brother's kids. She also looked after the children of her sister Kathy, Lavon's momma. She told them both, Pick up your kids Sunday because I have to work at the church on Monday morning, but neither of them got their kids, so they stayed with Jesenda and put her in a bind because she couldn't leave to clean the church. Miz Dolores told her not to worry: Just come on Tuesday, she said. But that's not the point. Jesenda's brother and sister didn't even apologize. Family will always take advantage.

Jesenda watches Lavon sulking in a chair. He crosses his arms and refuses to look at her. Miz Deborah Lacey, Mayo's momma, is his grandmomma. Her son Jerome is his daddy. He looks just like Jerome. The square jaw and deep-set eyes. Her daughter Taylor was fathered by ReShaun "Pee-Wee" Cunningham, the half-brother to Jerome and Mayo. Pee Wee got shot in the foot. He wasn't doing nothing, just standing around and a drive-by happened. He wasn't involved in no criminal activity. She's not with him anymore but she'll take up for him. She won't criticize him for something that wasn't his fault. He'll come by in his pickup and talk to her at the church but she doesn't encourage him, because she doesn't want her current boyfriend, Melvin, to think something's going on.

Jesenda notices a cobweb and swipes it with a rag. Pee Wee's a good daddy, she'll give him that. He stays involved with Taylor. He was eighteen or nineteen when Jesenda met him. They had known each other for nine months when she became pregnant with their first baby. The infant died in childbirth. Jesenda was seventeen. Didn't have a heartbeat. She felt abandoned by God. Why would He do this to her? It still bothers her, especially on the baby's birthday, May 7. She didn't blame herself. She just couldn't figure out what happened. She had done all that she was supposed to do. She didn't drink or do drugs. She made all her doctor appointments. Why would God want to take something from her that was so precious, something that would love her for being her?

Pee Wee was in jail at the time. He and some man got into it and the man said Pee Wee robbed him. He didn't have proof but Pee Wee didn't have proof he didn't, and he got locked up for a few months. Innocent until proven guilty, but really it's guilty until proven guilty, Jesenda thinks. He came down hard on her for their baby's death. A lot of stuff she tries to forget about him. He wasn't that bad a person, just not very thoughtful. Then they had Taylor. Pee Wee stays in her life. He gets upset when she doesn't keep good grades. That's more than most daddies. Too many men are sorry fathers, for real. They don't want to be involved in their child's life. They're trifling. A lot of fathers think that if they ain't with the momma they ain't with the child, but that's not right. They can be abusive, manipulative, and controlling. They say what they say to a woman to get her where they want her: in the bed. They don't care after that. She and Melvin have been together going on four years. A lot of relationships don't get beyond four minutes. He's not perfect. He always complains about the bills. He works for a construction company pouring concrete forty hours a week, but he has three kids of his own and has to pay child support, and that hurts since she works at the church only once a week. She understands, but their relationship has too much drama, too much stress, too much arguing. Even when money is tight, it shouldn't have to always be about money. He never does spontaneous things for her but what man does? Men don't think to do stuff like that for women. Jesenda wonders why. They don't see it growing up, she assumes. Every girl dreams of having flowers delivered for no reason. It doesn't have to be on her birthday or on Valentine's Day. Just out of the blue, or cooking dinner instead of waiting for her to do it, or walking together holding hands. Women like that. Melvin says, That's kiddy stuff. No it's not. None of her babies' daddies did that. Never in all her relationships. Never, ever, ever.

Your little cleaning service ain't doing nothing, Melvin told her.

I'm going to show you little, baby, she said. I'm going to show you how big little can be.

Get a job, he snapped back.

—◦◦◦—

Lavon lets out a long sigh and Jesenda tells him to hush up but she was no different at his age. She had a temper and could put on as good a pout as the next person when she wanted. She didn't appreciate being told nothing. The only people she listened to outside of her family were Mr. John and Miz Dolores, and sometimes not even them, not when she was really worked up. She has known them since she was a child. In those days, everyone called her "Nay-Nay" after Sheneneh Jenkins, a character that comedian Martin Lawrence created and voiced on his 1990s sitcom, *Martin*. Her happiest childhood memories revolve around the ministry. Light of the Village gave her access to another world, like she wasn't in the Village no more. She loved the six-week church summer camp. Mr. John and Miz Dolores would take the children on field trips. Before she became involved with the church, Jesenda would throw rocks at abandoned houses and bust out streetlights late at night. Things she knows now that she had no business doing.

She grew up in Prichard. Her momma died from a stroke when she was eight, and her daddy passed away a few years later from a massive heart attack. They both drank, used drugs, and suffered from high blood pressure. After her momma passed, Jesenda lived with an auntie on Eight Mile, an incorporated community named for its distance from Mobile, but she missed her momma.

Jesenda keeps pictures of her family on her phone. There. That's her auntie. Kind of blurred but that's her in the white, dappled dress. This next one is of her daddy, a large, bald man with a thin mustache. He wears a yellow shirt and tie, and a black jacket with wide lapels, and he looks into the camera with an impenetrable stare. This picture here is a cousin, Joe "Lil Joe" Johnson. He hangs out with rappers and organizes their security. He always has money. His Instagram account shows him with dollar bills rising from the floor to his waist. He and Jesenda went through juvenile detention at the same time, and that bonded them because they were so different from everyone else: They'd been to jail. She can't remember what Lil Joe had done but she's glad now that she survived that period of her life.

Everybody thought she and Lil Joe were brother and sister

because they had the same eyes. His momma would babysit her when her momma was out partying. She spent many days with Lil Joe coming up. One night while her auntie was out on an errand, she and her cousin "Buddy Buddy" snuck out of the house to buy candy. Four-year-old Lil Joe ran across the street after them, got hit by a car, and ended up with a broken leg. Oh, he cried so bad. Jesenda and Buddy Buddy were about eight years old. They panicked and left him by the side of the road because they weren't supposed to be outside. The driver called Lil Joe's momma. Everybody knew everybody. Oh, I accidentally hit your baby. It wasn't a big deal. Adults understood how to handle stuff without going off. It wasn't about, Oh you hit my baby, you fixin' to go to jail. Handling stuff meant Jesenda and Buddy Buddy got a whooping. Lil Joe spent two days in a hospital. Jesenda's auntie and Lil Joe's momma would visit him, come home, and say, We're still mad at y'all. Lil Joe got hit by that car trying to follow y'all. It hurt Jesenda's feelings to have her auntie mad at her but she understood the thought behind her anger: There's a reason adults tell you not to do stuff, a lesson she tries to instill in her kids.

When Lil Joe came home his momma put him in her bed which she kept high off the ground. He couldn't get off it for nothing because he had a cast on and it was so high. Anything he wanted, Jesenda got for him because she felt so bad. She helped him to the floor when he had to use the bathroom. As they grew older, Buddy Buddy always joked with her about the accident. Lil Joe never talked much about it.

After Lil Joe graduated from high school, he went off to make money on the street. He didn't want to struggle. He was tired of struggling. His personality hasn't changed now that he has money, but he hangs with people most everyone in the

Village doesn't know. He throws his kids the best birthday parties. Parties most people can't afford to give their children. He wanted money, and now he has it. He tells her it feels good to wake up in the morning knowing he can pay his bills.

Jesenda scrolls through her phone to a photo of herself at six. She wears a white dress, her hair tied back. She thumbs through more pictures. Brothers, sisters, cousins. Stepsisters and nephews, a lot of people in Jesenda's family. Most of these old photos were taken long before she entered foster care at twelve. Staying with her aunt wasn't bad, but it wasn't good either. Jesenda wanted her momma and daddy but they were gone and she didn't understand why. Her momma had problems but she was the best momma she could be. Her daddy may have been a crack addict but he took care of her. When her momma passed out from drinking, he made sure Jesenda was fed, bathed, and ready for school. He told her not to use drugs. He didn't follow his own advice, but he recognized his mistakes and she loved him for it.

One morning when she was in the seventh grade, Jesenda got into a fight with a boy on a school bus. He said something nasty about her hair and they had words and began hitting each other. Jesenda was a fighter. She even had a fight at Light of the Village years later when she struck Pee Wee with a stick. To this day, Mr. John will ask, Hey Nay-Nay, you still got your stick? and she replies, I don't carry my stick anymore, Mr. John, I carry my broom and mop. I'm doing my cleaning business now.

Oh yes, she was a fighter. Even though she's changed, people remember how she was, and she was bad, she was horrible. She was a mean, little bitty something who didn't take nothing from nobody. She didn't care. Life was hard without her momma and daddy. The old folks had an expression: Why're you smelling yourself? It means you're acting like you think you're grown, like you can handle life, like you think your bad little self don't stink. She was real, real naughty. She had a big mouth and pretty much anything would come out of it, enough to make God blush.

The bus fight landed Jesenda in the James T. Strickland Youth Center in Mobile. She got detained again for stealing a necklace from a store. It was twelve dollars and something. So petty. In juvenile detention, she got into fights. She didn't like being told what to do. It wasn't harsh. It's not like Mobile County Metro Jail, but no one wants to be locked up. No one wants to be ordered around all day. No one wants to be told how long they can shower, eat, and sleep. No one wants to be sprayed for lice every other day, either. That stuff made her hair fall out. It burned so bad when it got in her eyes. She stayed in Strickland for six months before she was placed in foster care at fourteen. A court-appointed social worker supervised her. Her foster parents were good people but they expected her to follow their rules. You have to be at home by seven, they'd tell her, but she'd come in at nine. You're not my momma. You can't tell me what to do, Jesenda would snap at them.

Sometimes she would get a home pass to visit her auntie. A social worker would come to the house and knock on the front door when it was time to return to her foster parents. Jesenda would dash out the back. The social worker would eventually catch up with her and lock her down in Strickland or the Lee County Youth Development Center in Opelika. Eventually she was placed with another foster family. Jesenda went back and forth between Strickland and foster care until she turned eighteen and aged out. She didn't have a favorite foster family. Most of them didn't have children. One lady had a granddaughter. She was really nice.

—◠◠◠—

I'm looking for my big broom, the red one, she tells Lavon as she puts aside her mop and enters the room where he sits. I want to sweep all the corners out with the small broom and use the big broom to come on through and get the rest.

I ain't seen it, Lavon says, still sulking.

Jesenda opens a closet and finds the broom. She believes in herself. She believes in the people of the Village. She is one of them. She wants to be an example of how it's possible to move on. The trials of her life toughened her. She just has to elevate her business to a point where it will support her and her children. The people in the Village aren't always killing each other. Still, she would not choose to live here. It's no place to hang out and chill. As rebellious as she was, Jesenda could not help but notice how her foster families lived a different life. They knew peace and calm. They didn't shout at each other. They didn't get angry and want to shoot someone. They looked forward to each day. She doesn't want her children to grow up amid chaos and violence and experience the kinds of losses she has. Her brother was shot at twenty-three. A bullet took the life of a close friend, but he had killed somebody. You live by it; you die by it. The other day, she had intended to see one of her sisters who was seven months pregnant and having a birthday party but she didn't make it. Just as well. There had been a shooting next door and a bullet entered her sister's house. Jesenda doesn't think her sister was a target, but a bullet don't care where it goes. She has no clue who was shooting or why. Neither does her sister. The bullet went through a window and all the way to a back bathroom. Didn't hit nobody, thank God. Jesenda just wishes the shootings would stop. All she can do is cry, stay strong for her kids, focus on her business, and pray to God, because no one else can fix it. She considers her life a success because she has lived this long when so many other people she knows haven't. She wants to teach her kids what she has learned about survival, and drill those hard earned lessons into them. Stuff they have to know. She shouldn't be gone and dead before they learn those kinds of basic things. She hates to think like that, but her momma and daddy left her at a young age. Her momma hadn't taught her all that she needed to know as a woman. She doesn't know when her time will come. When she dies, she hopes people speak well of her. She may not be good every day, but she wants to be known for being a nice person and a good momma who was close to God. She would like to live longer than twenty-eight.

Lavon, I'm tired of looking at you feeling sorry for yourself.

He stares at the floor, arms folded across his chest.

You helped me yesterday, Jesenda says. I'll pay you for that.

He looks up and smiles.

Now help me finish.

He starts sweeping the bathroom again. When he finishes, she hands him the mop and he cleans the floor. She takes the mop from him and lugs the bucket of dirty water outside and pours it into the street, watches it foam at her feet before it flattens and pools around a clogged sewer drain.

12

Jesenda puts the bucket away and leaves the church with Lavon. Bigg Man drives past. She watches him. He always cruises around. The way he treats people gets on her nerves. Makes them feel low by busting them on social media. He ain't no bad person, he does nice things but she doesn't like the way he disses people on Facebook because he has money. The way he flashes it. Lil Joe flashes but doesn't diss. We all came from the Village, she thinks. Money or no money, he ain't no different.

A car stops at the ministry and a young man, Aaron Amison, gets out. As a child he fed his grandmama's goats, and from that day forward everyone called him, Billy Boy. Remaining in the car is his pregnant girlfriend and the driver, one of Billy Boy's homeboys, whom he's convinced to take his girlfriend to the doctor for a checkup after dropping him off at the ministry. If they have a girl, Billy Boy thinks he will name her Nola. He can imagine her bad little self getting on his nerves. So he thought, Nola, for no you don't.

Girl, I just came from D block and I just seen your name on the wall of this empty house, Billy Boy says. It said, Nay-Nay and Shana

Where?

At the end of a house.

I don't know what house you talking about, Jesenda says.

Dolores steps out of the church to get a bag of toys from her car.

Hey, You look happy, Billy Boy says to her.

Yes, I am. I decided I wasn't dealing with my hair anymore so I got it cut last night.

Good look, good look. OK, OK, you're in the game.

Thank you. So you're here because your girlfriend needs a ride?

Yes, ma'am, but she found one.

Oh, good. Who is your girlfriend? Do I know who she is?

You haven't met her yet. Nobody has.

OK, Dolores says.

Brianna's her name.

Pretty name. Is that her there?

Dolores turns, faces the car where Brianna sits, and waves.

Hey, Brianna.

Brianna looks up. Billy Boy gives a nervous laugh. He has three children—ages ten, four, and two—in state custody. He needs to find a nice little apartment and a job to persuade the court to give them to him. Their mother is in trouble over drugs and Billy Boy has been in and out of prison. It doesn't matter what kind of a job. Billy Boy's good at whatever. More of a handyman type of guy, for real. He enjoys lifting and moving stuff. An active job, that would be good, something to tie him up all day. In 2019, Billy Boy had work with a company that installed tents and booths for fairs and concerts, but then the tailgate of a truck collapsed on his right hand and Billy Boy lost the job, received disability, and hasn't worked since. He supposes he'll have to apply for a job somewhere outside of the Village. Ain't no work in Prichard.

He notices Da'Cino crossing the street from the Light House. Da'Cino lifts his chin acknowledging Billy Boy and walks over.

What you doing? Early for you, Billy Boy.

What you talking about? Rained last night.

I know.

Warming up.

Around five o'clock it'll get cold again, Da'Cino says.

They say it's going to stay warm.

You know how it is down here. Be warm; at five it be cold.

I want to get me a bike, man, Billy Boy says. Spandex, little gym shorts. Skinny, tight kind.

I thought you wanted shoes for your birthday.

Doing it all, man.

Where would you ride?

Nowhere. I'd have a picture of it on my phone. Just to show everybody I got one.

Ride with it on top of a car, Da'Cino says.

Just for show. Me and my bike are going out.

Tell some dude, Let me see your bike, man.

And never bring it back, Billy Boy says. I got you, man. Just for an hour.

And don't bring it back.

Come back and all the wheels are gone.

Man, it didn't have tires when you gave it to me, Da'Cino says, imitating Billy Boy.

They both bust up laughing. Da'Cino walks into the church and Billy Boy wanders down Baldwin following its tilted slabs of paving and the contortion of tree roots pushing through the cracks. He passes the ruins of an old house, a fireplace stands among fallen bricks. Sparrows perch on the broken chimney. A red pickup pulls alongside him and Billy Boy recognizes the large man behind the wheel as a producer of local rappers.

What up, Sheridan?

Billy Boy, where you been, man?

I've been busy.

I been wanting to get you in the studio, man.

I've been meaning to call you. I'm ready.

We gotta drop some tapes, Sheridan says.

I'll try to get it together.

Look up Jack Harlow. He be dropping. White boy. He's different. His beats are just different.

I love your beats, man, Billy Boy says.

We'll be talking then.

Awright.

Bill Boy watches him drive away. He believes he could earn big money rapping. Cats around here know he has talent, but he doesn't trust studios. Producers have hidden agendas because they're so thirsty to work with him and he has nothing—no name, no money—so that makes him think there's a catch. They might get his lyrics, give him a little money, and make a fortune. It's a lawyer thing. Too many guys can buy lawyers but Billy Boy ain't into all that. Money can't turn him. If he likes you, nobody can pay him to dislike you. They can't buy his loyalty. His loyalty comes from sweat and blood, it comes from the street. Billy Boy doesn't have time for no games. If produced right and orchestrated right, his raps would be a success. What he says is earned. What he says is true, collected from the experiences of his life. He doesn't need to be all flash like Bigg Man. Yeah, we know you got money, Bigg Man, everybody knows it. Your clothes, your cars, and all. The grillz. Billy Boy could be flashing too if he wanted, but his flash is in his words, not in jewelry. He does a lot of walking, rapping to himself without paper or pencil. Freestyling. Gives him peace of mind. He raps to keep calm. His words provide him with a chance to tell his story, and the streets can vouch for its authenticity. All he needs to do is make that jump into production with someone he can trust.

He will turn twenty-eight in a few days. A lot of years, man, a lot of years, for real. Maybe not for the pretty people in Mobile and the suburbs, but for him and his homeboys, yeah, a lot of years. The pretty people have no knowledge and mostly no interest in a brother like him. He doubts any of them would be surprised to see their twenty-eighth birthday. They're much too judgmental. They're like Bigg Man with their cars and money. Billy Boy believes he has life skills to teach them. Mr. John and Miz Dolores, they know. They're pretty people but they came to the Village because they understood not everybody has money. In the outside world, the universe of pretty people, when someone falls, they panic. Unlike Billy Boy and everyone he knows, they ain't used to not having. People in the Village, man, know struggle. They were raised on struggle and not having. If they fall, they know how to pick themselves up and live by scraping bottom, because the bottom, man, has been home for a long time. This right here, the weeds and the cuts Billy Boy follows throughout the Village, teaches survival. The people who are up now and living high should come down to where Billy Boy lives and learn something about it. Learn about living down. He can show them how they can make it without nothing and how they can be hungry and see another day and get on with little. Little is good. That's a good day to have little. If you have little, then you got something, and something is better than nothing because nothing don't fill no empty stomachs. One day, the pretty people may ask for his help. They might be so far down they'll need to sleep in an abandoned house with no roof. The apocalypse, man, that's what it would be like for the pretty people. He can teach them how to persevere without power, without water, without plumbing, for real, or anything to piss and bathe in. It's no big deal. Make it through that and anything above it will feel better—feel like you're kicking back with the big dogs. He wishes the pretty people would open their hearts and try to understand him. He is so curious about them and what they do. Just their normal life, man, for real. Do they go fishing with their kids? Do they wake up every day with their entire family and not find that strange? What is it like to assume you'll wake up the next day, that you'll even have a next day? Billy Boy doesn't know anyone who has that kind of peace. A typical day for people Billy Boy knows would be: Get your guns, get your dope; not, OK honey, I'm home, what's for dinner? Just a day or two around people like that would be different. To be a child growing up with all the trimmings, Billy Boy would have loved that. Like a fantasy, man, that kind of security. To be held and hugged and loved. To call your momma and have her answer. Year after year he would have celebrated his birthday and received gifts and taken it all for granted. Be tripping just thinking about it, for real. Areas outside of the Village seem like another country. Mobile might as well be Paris. When he leaves the Village he operates like he's underwater. By that he means he shields himself, he tries to go unnoticed, low-key as possible, so he can return to the Village without nobody stopping him, retreat to one of these empty houses and chill and sit for what remains of the day, and think of who lived here once and what life was like for them. He might just find a pair of jeans or Nikes and stash his shit and leave out to come back later. A safe place for his stuff. A home. Have to clean up the place. So many houses could be fixed up, but people got to want them. Don't nobody care for them. If it weren't for Billy Boy checking up on these houses and running off the crackheads, he thinks someone would just burn them.

Man, if he had some money he'd really make these houses look nice. He'd have him a kitchen. He can cook. In jail, he would make his own birthday cake. He took a honey bun, two Reese's Peanut Butter Cups, some M&M cookies, and put it all in a bowl, mixed in water, milk, heated it, and watched it rise. A cup of noodles on the side, and that was his birthday. Maybe he could work at a bakery. He wants a new pair of shoes, a nice pair. Need them for a job interview. Billy Boy's Bakery. He laughs. He wants what Bigg Man has, for real, but he doesn't want to be flashy like Bigg Man. He doesn't need to be drawing motherfuckers to him like that. People crowd him. A pair of kicks would lift his spirits. The pretty people would look at his shoes and think he was sharp.

What would he tell the pretty people about himself? He thinks he'd start with his arrest at thirteen for carrying a gun. A friend gave it to him. They had exchanged words with some guys in the Village. Billy Boy was younger than his friend, but he had heart so his partner gave him the weapon. Watch your back, Billy Boy, don't let nobody do nothing to you. A .22, a little thing. The police jumped out and caught him with it one day when he was walking down D block toting it like a gangster. A judge sent him to Strickland. His momma didn't bother to come to court. He served thirty days before he was transferred to a group home in Dothan. He kept to himself.

He was new, quiet, and avoided trouble. He slipped out one night through an open door when everyone was asleep and the guards weren't paying attention. He didn't know where he was going. He walked and walked into the next night without being stopped. He didn't sleep. Just kept stepping and hitch-hiking. Had to keep moving until he reached Prichard. Since then he has been back inside a few times. For robbery in 2012 and 2014, and robbery and assault in 2016. See if he can stay out this time.

The wrong crowd, man, and not being patient will put a man in prison, Billy Boy knows. For some reason he had the drive to steal, to do something and get away with it. Even when he had money he would still rob a brother and break into houses. The rush was thrilling, being high and the seclusion of the Village made it easy. Don't nobody care about who do what in here. The police don't control it. As a kid he thought he could do anything and no one would hurt him because he was young. Who's going to kill a boy for robbing them? Then he saw kids his age and younger getting hurt and he realized, OK, they will shoot a child; they will kill that child: boy or girl, it don't matter. He watches over his shoulders. He walks the paranoid path because he knows what he did when he was younger and the folks he did it to, and they are still out here.

A side of him can get uncontrollably angry. Mean angry. Scary angry. He tries not to let that side out. If someone attempted to harm him, if he felt pushed against the wall, for real, then, hell yeah, he'd hurt that person. But it scares him, that kind of anger. People who have never seen him angry wouldn't look at him the same if they saw him lose his temper. He can get hot pretty quick and can be hard and straightfor-ward with his words and his fists and guns, for real, whatever is required. He has had his hands involved in a few shootouts but no one died. He thanks God for that. The Village can't do nothing for him except turn his life into something he doesn't want it to be. That's why he has to be careful. He wrestles with his temper and his attitudes. Ain't no sense in him being out in the streets holding the road because the streets are deadly. Bring the worst out of him.

He copes through prayer. All he does is pray. It's not on-top-of-a-roof praying, but it's prayer. He prays for his safety, his family's safety. He prays to God that he has the wisdom to identify danger. When he was in jail, he prayed with other guys. They had faith to a certain extent, but too many of them lost it when they got out. The world of faith ain't the world of the 'hood. Billy Boy tattooed a cross between his eyes. Every time he looks in a mirror he sees it as a reflection of his love for God.

He wants to preach, eventually. Get him something like Mr. John, Miz Dolores got going on. That's the only reason he can see that God has allowed him to live this long. God wants him to do something. There have been times when Billy Boy has been submissive to death. Like man, this is it. I give up. I ain't going to make it. But then this voice in his head pops up: You can't die. How you going to give up when you have children to feed? How you going to give up when you got a calling? When you got a destiny? It's not written for Billy Boy to give up. God has confirmed his fate.

Billy Boy stops by a car parked in the driveway of an abandoned home and buys a cigarette for fifty cents from the dude behind the wheel. He smokes, looks around. He stands on Escambia Street. Follow it one way and he'll reach Dunlap Circle. Follow it another way it stops at a dead end near Bigg Man's crib. The roads branching off of it all buried under trash and brush. Those are the backstreets where the old cats come, start a fire in a barrel, and drink a lot of wine. Don't do much but drink. Billy Boy is one of the youngest of the old cats. Not many old school players left. If he doesn't find them here, he'll find them at a hit house kicking back and drinking dollar shots of liquor. Those are his spots too. Hole-in-the-wall juke joints. A mature crowd. Chill, drink-a-shot-or-two type of guys. Billy Boy doesn't worry about them. They won't go off into nonsense and shoot their friends. Billy Boy prefers them to younger cats. He needs to slow down. He needs to pray. Pray for new shoes. Pray really hard to be successful. Pray to resist his worst impulses. He doesn't want to make any more mistakes.

13

Morgan Copeland, a Light of the Village staff member, walks into the church. She greets Dolores and checks her phone calendar to see which clients she'll see today. She grew up in Enterprise, Alabama, about 160 miles east of Prichard and never expected to work in the Village. She had never heard of it until she attended the University of Mobile as a music major.

In the fall of 2007, during her freshman year, a college friend invited her to lead a music class at Light of the Village. Morgan had no idea Prichard existed. It's hard now for her to remember what drew her back. The kids, she thinks. How they thrived with just minimal attention. John and Dolores too. Their quiet yet determined belief in their mission. But it was difficult. She didn't understand street slang and had never experienced the kinds of losses the children had. She doesn't recall feeling shocked but assumes she was.

At a recent Bible study with half a dozen teenagers, Morgan said women should not have children outside of marriage. That hit a nerve. Not one child in the room had parents who had been wed. How does she express her beliefs without sounding accusatory? How does she raise uncomfortable topics? She has worked with these kids for years. When she considers that they come from generations of single mothers and absent fathers, she feels overwhelmed. She hopes that the children will find an alternative to violence. Not getting shot. Not committing a crime. Making a choice to leave the street. Those feel like basic, achievable goals. Then perhaps college, a job, and a two-story home. For the next generation, or the generation after that.

She is careful not to overstep, not to expect them to behave a certain way just because she thinks they should. They make their own choices. Some young people choose to sell drugs, no matter how many times she says: Hey, you need a plan. What are you going to do? Let us help you. She asks questions hoping they'll begin to think of alternatives, and stays involved without judgment.

During the COVID-19 quarantine, she ran into a young man who said he was going to be a dad and he was pretty excited about it. Although he accepted the responsibility, he had no idea of the difficulties he'd be facing. He'd need a job to support his baby and the mother, and he'd need transportation to that job. If he wanted a good job, he'd need a trade and that would require an education. She doesn't think he and other young fathers intend to avoid responsibility. They're thrilled by the prospect. They just don't understand what's involved because of their youth and their experience growing up without fathers.

Most people would assume that pregnancy at such a young age would be a crisis, but most of the teenage girls Morgan knows are as excited as the fathers. They act a little self-conscious when they tell her but not upset. She has learned that if she spoils that moment, they will remember and shut her out. It's not worth it. They're pregnant. It's already done. What

is there to do other than commend them and support them?
She doesn't think she has to go over the top. We're so proud,
congratulations, nothing like that, but she shouldn't scold.
Show interest. Help them prepare for the responsibility. Stay
involved. It's hard. It's a very fine line and she doesn't always
know where to draw it and when she can cross it.

Were Raven and Terika both pregnant at the same time?
Morgan asks Dolores.

Yes, they were.

Raven was fourteen and pregnant and Terika was fifteen, right?

Both pretty young, Dolores says.

Exceptionally young. My first summer here other than
teaching music this is what stands out. Raven was big pregnant. Not so much Terika.

Was Raven's baby Dee Tee's child?

Was it?

I think. At least one of them.

OK, Morgan says. You're saying Raven and Dee Tee and
then she had another baby with Jodeci. He died in 2015.

No, 2013.

His baby's name is also Jodeci. They call him Gucci, Morgan
says.

Yes.

Jodeci the father was shot.

Morgan stretches, running her hands through her hair. It
gets confusing keeping all their names straight. Her friends
and family can't fathom why she works for the church. She
couldn't either if she were them. She thinks a tornado that
swept through Enterprise on March 1, 2007, influenced her.
Her mother worked in a hospital and took her out of school
that day because the forecast predicted rough weather.

About one o'clock an EF-4 tornado struck the city and the high school with winds of up to 170 miles an hour. Eight students died. Morgan knew four of them. She approached the injured in the emergency room and offered to pray. It was the first time she had experienced the sudden loss of people so young. It didn't prepare her for what she has seen in the Village, but it may have given her the ability to cope with tragedy in ways she still doesn't understand. There is no getting used to losing people so young.

A couple of middle school girls she picked up the other day for the after-school program said, I hope there's a fight in school tomorrow. What? Morgan said. Yeah, because school is boring. One girl said she seeks thrills and excitement in life. Middle-class kids say that too, but for this girl and many others that Morgan knows, opportunities to play in an amusement park or travel or do other fun things don't exist, so they seek entertainment elsewhere. Watching fights at school shouldn't be it, however. She wonders what compels them toward violence. Is it more exciting than everyday life? Have their brains become addicted to it like a drug? The rush of shootings, fights, people arguing. Is it the same as a traffic accident when drivers slow down to stare?

Morgan thinks Jesenda may be part of a new generation that thinks differently—if her business succeeds. She will need to adhere to a schedule and remain disciplined. Be on time, be professional, make sure she has someone to look after her kids. Do all that, avoid discouragement—or at least not let it hold her back—and get new clients.

Over the years, Morgan has noticed a kind of passivity people have toward disappointment and hopes Jesenda does not succumb to that. The homeless man, Mr. Tommie, may be one of the most passive. He spends his days collecting trash to recycle, but looking for a job is not even plan B with him. Sixty-four years old; he gets up at dawn. He doesn't laze around. Going to a job every day would be far easier than searching for cans and gathering firewood. He can work but he has to believe he can and want to. He cared for his mother in her final years, and then she died and he turned to the street. Like there were no other options. Perhaps his mother looked after him as much as he looked after her.

Self-advocacy is not even a concept. Morgan worked with one woman who needed her apartment door fixed after someone broke in. Get management on the phone and have them repair it, Morgan told her. It's a matter of safety. Tell them you are not paying rent until this is done. That ability to call and get answers. Ask until you get what you're after. It goes for housing, jobs, health care, dealing with school. In all ways, self-advocacy is lacking. Poverty, drugs, gun violence, all of that plagues the Village and Prichard in general but the number one thing that afflicts the community, Morgan believes, is apathy. Number one. How does she advocate for someone if they don't have the drive to do it themselves or at least ask her to help them do it? But then if someone does have the drive, they may not have the words to communicate without anger. The ability to articulate a thought beyond emotion—the ability to say: I need this handled today or I'll file a complaint or withhold rent or whatever—and the confidence to say that. Almost like a child afraid to speak up in class. Not enough confidence in their skills, their voices, to speak for themselves.

Mr. Tommie behaves like that. She sees him differently than other men who ask for two bucks every day. Many of them live in government housing and have a place to wash their clothes and eat. Mr. Tommie doesn't and she wonders if he ever will. It's as if he thinks that if he leaves his little corner of the world, his camp at the academy, he will fail and have nothing. He lives a hard life. Staying outside can't be easy. He chooses to scramble every day of his life. She doesn't know what to do with him.

Jesenda, on the other hand, appears to have confidence but she can be impulsive. She became frustrated with Morgan the other day when she told her that she couldn't clean on Sundays because the church would be closed after Bible study. Oh, so you don't trust me, Jesenda said. No, it's not a matter of trust, it's a matter of safety. She ended up coming to work that Tuesday morning before the church had opened. Da'Cino let her in. She had disregarded everything. Can't overstate my influence, Morgan reminds herself. She likes Jesenda but there's still a level of pushback, a kind of you-can't-tell-me-what-to-do attitude.

Morgan finds her job to be very isolating. Even her friends who think they understand what she does don't know. Not really. Going through her day and someone drops a bomb, Did you hear? So-and-so was shot last night. It just breaks her heart. Towns and cities issue storm alerts when a tornado approaches. The Village offers no warning. Death strikes like a hawk hunting its prey, with unexpected speed, shattering an otherwise calm day. Morgan carries the sorrow of their deaths but won't take responsibility for choices the dead may have made. She deals with the stories she hears, absorbing information like a sponge, wringing herself out when she gets home. She exercises at a gym. It's good therapy, eases her stress. She does what she can but the choices they make, they own. Whether they testify in court about an abusive boyfriend or get themselves into a detox program or shoot someone who insulted them or put in a job application or see a counselor, at the end of the day, she has no control over their decisions.

—⁓—

Twenty-six-year-old Patricia Hayward, a single mother of two, a boy and a girl, walks into the church and approaches Morgan. She wore her hair in ponytails as a girl and everyone called her "Pony," a nickname her friends and family still use. Morgan has arranged for her to meet an aircraft mechanic, Kevin, who offered to volunteer at the church and help people develop career goals. He sits in another room waiting to be introduced. Whatever advice he has to offer, Morgan thinks, Pony can use. She has trouble committing to goals. She jumps from one idea to the next: I'll go back to school. I'll start my own business. I'll join the military. I'll become a cop. I'll be a beautician. She has a job at a Walmart distribution center in Mobile and at Hart's Fried Chicken, a fast-food restaurant she has worked at off and on for years, but is dissatisfied with both.

How are you on this lovely morning, Pony? Morgan says.

It's nice but it don't know if it wants to be hot or cold.

It was cold this morning.

What you saying? I didn't want to come out of the house.

But you had to.

Life calls. I had to.

Morgan takes her to Kevin. He stands and they shake hands. He's dressed casually but professional in a blue dress shirt and slacks. Morgan explains to Pony that Kevin has stopped in to discuss her career goals.

Good, I need that, she says.

She follows him into a back room. He closes the door and Pony sits down. Kevin stands by a whiteboard and explains his background. He speaks with enthusiasm, as if he continues to be surprised by his own career trajectory, at his eventual success. As a young man, he says, he drove trucks. Then he joined the army during the Gulf War. After the war, he left the military and became a lead mechanic at the Mobile Aeroplex at Brookley Field.

At first I did want to go into the army, but I got kids, Pony says.

Pony had her first child, Natalia, when she was thirteen. Too soon, she admits. It wasn't supposed to happen. At the time, she and her siblings stayed with her grandmomma behind what used to be Tony's Seafood on Highway 45 in Mobile. The owner gave Pony's momma credit because he understood times were hard. Pony watched a lot of TV after school until her momma insisted she get out of the house. Enjoy the sunlight, girl! She hung with her friends on D block and that's when she met Natalia's daddy. Young, dumb, and just wanting to live life, that was me, she tells Kevin. She panicked when she became pregnant. Asked the doctor how she could kill the fetus forming inside her. The doctor looked at her like she was crazy and told her momma. Her momma said, No, girl, you're having this baby. Her momma had the upper hand back then.

She didn't understand the changes to her body, just knew she had another life filling her. Schoolkids called her a freak, a whore, but then a couple of them became pregnant so they had to shut up, for real. The demands on her life didn't change because she was pregnant. She had to wake up before six thirty in the morning to be sure and catch the school bus. Ain't there on time, the driver be gone. She didn't play, she ain't waiting, she ain't doing nothing but her job, and Pony soon realized that walking to school pregnant was no joke.

That's why I wanted to share my path, Kevin tells her. You need to write a resume. You may not know the endgame but you have life experiences that can contribute to a job. You look at your circumstances and what's possible and then develop short-term goals and work toward them. Another door may open toward bigger goals.

Right, Pony says. I've basically been at Hart's for five years and now I've been at Walmart for two years. I got to find something else. I don't know where to start or where to go no more.

Her momma helped her after Natalia was born. Pony had no idea how to be a parent. She dropped Natalia off at a day care center before school, and walked from school to pick her up in the afternoon and waited until her momma got there after work and took her home.

You might be able to go back to school.

I don't know if that's what I want, Pony says.

Natalia's daddy never comes around. In her experience most men don't want to be daddies, not in a for-real way. They don't care to grow up and be responsible for someone they helped create. They still want to live their life, but they brag when they're around their homeboys: Oh, this is my child. Natalia's daddy even denied being her father. He was afraid he'd be accused of statutory rape.

She was twenty-one when she became pregnant with Cordell, her son, now four. At the time, she had dropped out of . Bishop State Community College. She had been enrolled on a basketball scholarship but didn't keep up her grades. Depressed and hanging out on D block, she met Cordell's daddy. He was smooth and spoke all kinds of comforting words.

He stayed with Pony but they argued so much she told him to leave. He said she was a crybaby. She just needed attention. He didn't have a job, he didn't do nothing while she worked every day. Feet all swole up, body swole up, cooking chicken at Hart's; big belly and everything. Her manager told her, You need to stop working. You're going to end up popping on the job. Her water broke two days later. Cordell's daddy watched him every day for a while but as he got older he didn't want nothing to do with him.

A lot of women expect to meet a man who'll stick around, but they never do. Women always get the low-down dirty son of a gun, Pony believes. Men show the sweet innocent side until their true colors shine through, but by then the women have already become attached. The men be so nice and talk to a woman and listen to her until they get what they want and then they're done with her..

I have to find one job that fits for me and my family, Pony says. I don't want to stay here. I'm sick of the Village. I'm sick of Mobile. I see the same old thing every day. I feel like I'm getting nowhere.

You should look at jobs that accommodate family, Kevin says. Federal jobs are good for folks with families. Poke around, see if anything looks interesting.

I need to build an escape plan to get me and my kids out. I did want to go into the medical field, but I love cooking at the same time. I should go back to school and get a degree like you said. I don't know.

Do your research. There are so many opportunities.

Pony begins to cry. She tries to talk but can't. Kevin waits. Pony wipes her eyes.

I'm sure you came through some tough times, she says finally. How do you get through them?

I had a wife supporting me. She pushed me to keep moving forward.

I don't have that.

—◦◦◦—

Later that day, Pony returns to the church with Cordell. He enjoys playing on the swing set and slide. Pony sits at a picnic table and watches him. Kevin seemed nice enough, Pony thinks, but what he advised her to do would take too long. Do your research, he said, but where will she find the time to do that and find something long term while she works these dead-end jobs? She needs the long term now. Just hasn't figured out how to get it yet. She had hoped Kevin would have the answer.

Pony began coming to Light of the Village when John and Dolores started summer Bible camp in 2003. She was about eight years old and remembers wondering, Who let the white folks into the 'hood? No one expected white folks to have a church. She grew used to John and Dolores the more involved she became with their ministry. Everybody came: Bigg Man, Mayo, Billy Boy, the whole Village clique. Everyone used to hang out on D block. Teenagers and some younger kids. Everyone got along. Everyone knew everybody, and everyone would notice if a regular was absent, because everybody stayed on the street or went to the church. At that time, people weren't going head-to-head with each other, nobody was killing nobody. If they did, it was really unexpected. Pony doesn't see much of Bigg Man now that he's king of the 'hood. He has too much going on. Too hot. She can't be around that. She doesn't want her kids around that. And D block is nothing but woods now.

But when they were younger Bigg Man, Billy Boy, Mayo, and everybody for real were just goofy kids having fun at the church. Mr. John was always pretty easygoing with everybody, but Pony learned fairly quickly that Miz Dolores didn't play. She got on Pony a few times. When Miz Dolores pulled her aside, Pony listened. She had pretty much grown up with this little white woman. Miz Dolores had been her teacher but when she got in trouble Miz Dolores talked to her like she was her momma and Pony listened.

You OK, Cordell?

Yes, momma.

Watching him play, she remembers a mission trip Mr. John organized to Juárez, Mexico. She, Da'Cino, and about a dozen other kids from the church participated. They flew from Pensacola, Florida, to El Paso, Texas. She had never been on a plane and as it climbed, she screamed, and a flight attendant closed her window shade so she couldn't see how high they were. Oh, Lord, here we go, Pony thought. When the plane banked, Pony worried it was falling out of the sky.

They drove from El Paso to Juárez. The distant mountains impressed her. So solitary and bare except for some trees that appeared farther away than the mountains. Pony and the other kids helped build houses out of sand and bricks. She spent a lot of time with mommas of small children and babies. She couldn't speak a word of Spanish—the women spoke too fast for her to catch on—but she thought they understood her in the quiet way they smiled at her and gestured, encouraging her to join them for a meal. She played soccer with the Mexican boys, but they played as fast as they spoke and she got beat up a little bit. At the end of the weeklong trip, Pony concluded that the people in Juárez had even less than families in the Village. They experienced a different kind of struggle from anything she knew. No roads, nothing but dirt. See a couple dogs but little else. They used whatever materials were available to build their houses. No one in the Village built their own house. The children walked farther than she ever did to catch a school bus. They struggled alone. No Section 8 in Mexico. No gunshots out there, either, despite all the things she had heard about drug cartels. Pony noticed the silence but it didn't disturb her. Sometimes it got quiet in the Village too, but it was a quiet that eventually broke into violence. In Juárez, the silence extended as far as the mountains, even beyond. She wondered if maybe she did hear gunshots but had become so accustomed to them in the Village that she just didn't notice. Odd to think of no gunshots at all.

Pony doesn't dream about violence, but the feeling she gets when she approaches a dead body is like a dream. That feeling of being scared but not scared. She just walks up to it and looks. It's not new. She ran the streets and saw dead bodies when she was a child. She'd hear gunshots and just walk over and check it out. It was shocking because the dead often looked asleep but she could always feel something missing. Just something that told her this person wasn't asleep. No movement. No sound. Not even a sniffle. Even a sleeping person moves. Eyelids flutter. They fidget. Something. She wanted to be sure the dead person wasn't family. That's what matters. When she hears about a shooting now, she asks who got hurt. Who died? Was it my cousin, my momma, my brothers, anybody? She makes calls and accounts for everybody. Frantic, heart racing.

Are they OK? Are they alive? It terrifies her to think it might be one of her own.

Pony hasn't had a stable home since her momma's house burned down in 2020 just before Christmas. Neighbors said it was from the dryer but the day before some woman told Pony's momma she was going to torch her house because she thought her momma had been talking smack about her behind her back. I'm going to bring your house down; and the next day the house burned. Her momma and her brother moved in with Pony in Gulf Village. It reminded her of the families she'd seen in Mexico. People on the floor, in beds, in chairs, whatever was available. Her grandmomma once told her that two grown people can't stay in the same house because they're going to have different opinions about how everything should be done, and she was right. Pony and her momma had words.

Are you doing OK, Cordell?

Yes, momma.

Cordell runs with both of his arms out like an airplane and leaps into the air. He likes to play Spider Man. His teacher in pre-K calls him a good kid. When he was born, the doctor told Pony he would need speech therapy because he had a small tongue, but he talks fine. Doctors always give the worst case scenario. As long as he can talk, she'll be happy. He gets constipated real quick and when he does his intestines twist. At least that's how Pony understands it. Doctors want to do some kind of surgery but Pony hasn't agreed to it. She doesn't want anyone cutting on her son at such a young age. He takes medicine to help with his bowel movements and she watches what he eats and drinks. Look at him play. No one would ever know he has any problems. He can be more demanding than Natalia. Whatever he wants, he expects to get. Natalia is more laid back, but when she wants something she'll ask and ask and ask.

Natalia is twelve but so tall she looks older. About to become a teenager. Pony jokes that she will put tracking devices on all her clothes. Every time she thinks about Natalia going to high school, she asks herself, How old am I? What's going on? When did I become twenty-six? What the hell? Time does fly. It needs to slow down. The years drag her along like a leaf caught in the wind. She talks to Natalia about the mistakes she made, but the girl doesn't want to hear it. That scares Pony. I had you at a young age, I don't want you to make the same mistake. Goes in one ear and out the other. Natalia knows everything and Pony doesn't, but Pony persists. Better to hear it from her than the streets. The streets have no mercy. She tells her brothers, Don't bring guns to my house; don't come here smelling of weed. They respect the gun part, the weed stuff not so much. They all smoke it. Cordell comes to her and asks, What's that smell? Pony has to spray her house with deodorizer.

Her stepdaddy, Cornelius, or "Big C" as everyone called him, was a dope dealer. He kept his weed locked in a freezer, wrapped tight in black plastic bags. He did try to dial it down when he had kids with Pony's momma. He died of a heart attack in 2015. Pony remembers that day. He let her drive his pickup to get him some Red Hots candy but he didn't touch them when she brought them back. His blood pressure was sky-high. That night, she heard him snoring in a funny way like he was gasping for air. Her momma hollered to her, Call 911! Pony ran into the bedroom and administered CPR. The ambulance took an hour to arrive. She saw bubbles of saliva popping around Big C's mouth. He was short and fat in contrast to her real daddy, who stood six feet but he wasn't no real daddy to her, nothing more than a sperm donor to her momma. He didn't spend any time with Pony. Big C was there for her. The fact that he lies six feet under doesn't change that. He knew her since she was in diapers. Taught her how to cook, drive, change a tire, all that. She still visits his grave.

Cordell, that's enough now, let's go home.

Momma!

Don't momma me. Let's go.

He runs toward her, arms out and making sounds like he's flying. She stands. An acorn falls on the church dumpster, makes a sharp sound like a gunshot but Pony knows the difference and doesn't flinch.

14

As Pony gets in her car and leaves with Cordell, a man with two boys drives up to the church in a green SUV and parks. He takes a basketball from the back and he and the boys walk behind the church to the basketball court. The boys take turns shooting baskets but hit high on the backboard, the ball bouncing over their heads and they run after it, competing to reach it first. The shorter boy picks it up and begins dribbling, pushing against the other boy, who tries to block him. A burst of gunfire from the Donut Shop interrupts them, and they react instantly. The shorter boy runs to the driver's side of the SUV, ducks down and keeps moving until he crouches behind it, then creeps forward to the passenger side and opens the door. Another burst of gunfire. Keeping his head low, the boy scrambles inside. The other boy and the man run from the basketball court to the driver's door and get in. The man backs onto Baldwin Drive and speeds toward Barbour Drive, hangs a right and accelerates onto Dunlap Circle and follows it to Wilson Avenue. The sound of the SUV fades. One final burst of gunfire. Then nothing. The warm and lazy afternoon resumes without further distraction.

That evening, rain falls and the sky is pitch-black. The Village is so darkened that the few remaining hovels vanish in the night. Water collects on Baldwin Drive and begins rising. Regulars of the hit house get in their cars and drive on the church grounds to avoid the expanding lake while others barrel through it, raising vast wings of water until they reach higher ground, and still it rains bleak and impenetrable.

Days later, amid the croaking of frogs and chattering of insects, the muddy water remains rank and steaming under a hot sun.

PART TWO

1

Text message: *Hey Mr John dis Corey remember I wanna take you and Miz D out to eat—wherever u wanna go—I'm 4 real—let me kno—*

2

Throughout his life, John Eads has found guidance when he needed it most. He was born in Dallas, moved to El Paso at the age of five. He was the younger of two children. His older brother, Kevin, played football but performed poorly in school. He liked to draw and attended a backpacking camp in the summer. He began smoking marijuana as a teenager and after he graduated from high school, Kevin would lie around the house getting high. Over time, he began muttering to himself and behaving oddly. A psychiatrist eventually diagnosed Kevin as paranoid schizophrenic. John's parents divorced, adding to the tension between Kevin and his father who was a strict disciplinarian. He eventually kicked Kevin out of the house. Sometimes when John was in the car with his father they would see Kevin sleeping on a park bench. There's Kevin, his father would comment, and he would drive past and say nothing else. It always struck John as a little strange.

John was on his own delinquent path. The administration at El Paso Morehead Junior High School suspended him twice, the second time for flipping off his eighth-grade math teacher,

Ms. Driscoll when she had corrected him for talking in class. He could tell by the look on her face that she was more hurt than angry. She sent him to the principal's office and the school notified his father that John would be suspended for three days. Walking home that afternoon, John knew his father would be furious. He cleaned his room and the garage hoping to lessen his punishment. When his father came home, he said nothing to him. Instead, he took John to Jackson's Restaurant on North Mesa Street. This was not the response John had expected. He asked for Tampico-style steak and waited. His father was up to something, he knew. He didn't have to wait long. After the waitress took their order, John's father slid a pamphlet from the New Mexico Military Institute in Roswell across the table. The institute offered high school and junior college. His father didn't have to tell him that's where he was going, and John didn't object. In fact, he recalls feeling happy as he read the pamphlet. He needed something. Even at the age of fourteen, he understood he was at loose ends.

The institute tamed his rebellious spirit out of him, and he began to embrace structure. He learned what it meant to be responsible. If he didn't clean his room for inspection, the supervising officer would punish everyone in his squad and he would get the crap beaten out of him. He joined the boxing team, the only white kid on it. The Black coach introduced John to his Latino teammates and he learned how to connect with people whose lives were very different from his. He made friends. The coach called him his white son.

He also grew close to the chaplain, Vernon Edmondson. Kind and approachable, Edmondson always wore a smile. He encouraged cadets to read the Bible as a book of stories and not as a weighty tome. Take it, go off by yourself, he told them. The

book of John is a good place to start. He brought doughnuts to
Bible study, a nice touch, but for John and the boys, Edmond-
son's willingness to spend time with them meant much more.
He walked them through the Bible, story by story.

In March 1985, John found a note on his door to call home.
He was nineteen and knew something bad had happened. His
father had remarried by then and his stepmother told him
Kevin had been struck by a truck somewhere outside of Dallas
and killed. Just hit him head on. He had been surviving on the
street and sometimes stayed at a shelter where he got to know a
priest who identified his body. John took a bus home the next
day.

Kevin's death shook his father. For years he kept the clothes
Kevin had been wearing when he died. Decades later, John still
struggles to say how exactly his brother's death affected him.
It taught him that bad things can happen close to home. It
prepared him for unexpected and violent endings. He doesn't
think it influenced him to work with poor people; the Bible did
that. He wishes he had been a better brother, more supportive
of Kevin. The last conversation he had with him had been over
the phone. Kevin was convinced the devil was chasing him in
a Dallas 7-Eleven. That was weird. John doesn't know what he
could have said, but he regrets he didn't find the words to comfort his brother.

John completed his undergraduate degree at New Mexico
State University in Las Cruces. To support himself he took a
job in a jewelry store, where he met Dolores. They hit it off
immediately and liked to take long walks and play racketball.
They dated for three years before they married in May 1994,
a week after Dolores graduated from college with a degree in
special education.

About a year into their marriage, they moved to San Antonio, Texas, where John earned a master's degree in health care administration from Trinity University. In their off hours they devoted themselves to Christian ministry by volunteering with Prison Fellowship, the world's largest Christian nonprofit organization for prisoners, former prisoners, and their families. They also joined Angel Tree, a fellowship program that provides holiday gifts to children from their incarcerated parents. In addition, they helped with after-school and outreach programs, and organized Bible studies in housing projects for Victory Gospel, a Pentecostal/Deliverance church that offered help to the very poor. The compassion of its pastor, Donny Banks, and his wife, Jackie, impressed them. They didn't blame homeless people for their circumstances or require them to attend church. Instead, they offered help without conditions.

During the day, Victory Gospel staff and volunteers performed outreach in neighborhoods where people bought drugs. One afternoon they encountered a woman who appeared highly intoxicated but all they had to offer her was a piece of paper, a tract about how she could find Christ and shelter at Victory Gospel. This is not good, one of the staff said. She needs a meal. John and Dolores realized that if they were to establish their own ministry they would have to do more than share the Gospel. They would have to meet basic needs, and this prompted them to hand out hot dogs when they first came to the Village, they would recall that moment. Once they established their church, they began serving lunch once a week and breakfast on Sunday.

In 1996, John accepted a job with the Mobile Infirmary Health system in Mobile, Alabama. They joined a downtown church on Baltimore Street but left after three weeks because they didn't agree with the pastor's interpretation of the Bible, especially after one Sunday when a parishioner wanted to know if she'd see her mother again in heaven. No, you won't know each other in heaven, the pastor told her. His answer crushed her and contradicted the Apostle Paul in 1 Thessalonians 4:17: "We who are still alive will be caught up together with them in the clouds to meet the Lord in the air." John and Dolores also objected to the pastor's habit of sharing publicly how much each member tithed, as if it was a contest—or worse, an effort to shame people into giving more.

In December 2001, John and Dolores led Bible studies in Queens Court apartments, a housing project where a six-year-old boy had been killed and a Prichard police officer wounded in an ambush. Authorities said the shooting was in retaliation for the deaths of three young men by undercover officers. When Queens Court closed in May 2002, John and Dolores began looking at impoverished neighborhoods around Mobile to establish a ministry. By the time they drove through the Village, they had seen most of the city's housing projects but nothing had clicked. The Village did. The worn houses and overgrown yards and dark streets spoke of a desperate need.

In the following days, weeks, and months, John and Dolores walked through the Village speaking to families and offering them hot dogs. You guys aren't from here, people commented. John assumed they said that because he was white but now he thinks it's because they gave them food without conditions. This wasn't done in the Village. The hot dogs stimulated conversations. If someone asked for prayer, John would oblige them. He never suggested it himself. They could have a hot dog, but he wasn't shoving Jesus down anyone's throat.

No one was unpleasant, but they would all ask for money,

even the kids, and they could be aggressive. Hey, give me a dollar. That didn't happen in San Antonio. About half of the people they met in the Village were curious and asked questions, and about half of them said, You'll never last.

If we could start a ministry here, what would you want? John and Dolores asked. Children told them they wanted a place to play and people to take them on field trips. The adults were more subdued.

Yeah, they mumbled, a ministry would be good for the kids.

In 2002, John and Dolores bought a duplex on Baldwin for $7,500 to use as their church. An elderly man named Willie Allen owned it and several other properties, including a furniture store in the Prichard Mall. John and Dolores named their church Light of the Village, inspired by John 8:12: *Again Jesus spoke to them, saying, I am the light of the world. Whoever follows me will not walk in darkness, but will have the light of life," John and Dolores named their church Light of the Village.*

With help from a South Carolina ministry, they rehabilitated the house, plugging the gaping holes and shoring up the collapsed roof.

It's pretty messed up, one man told them.

Yeah, another man agreed, but the rafters are OK. You won't be here more than a couple weeks anyway.

Some kids broke in, trashed the building, and tried to set it on fire but a neighbor stopped them.

Light of the Village started with a small core of families. John didn't care about numbers. He reminded himself of Matthew 18:20: *For where two or three gather together as my followers, I am there among them.* The kids just showed up on their own. John doesn't remember a parent approaching him and asking if their son or daughter could participate. Bigg Man and Lawrence were among the first to get involved. They both had some heft but Bigg Man was distinctive. He had a scar on his face, a reminder of a run-in (literally) with a door long before John and Dolores knew him. He was a goofball, a boy full of fun but other kids were off the chain. Just wild. If he and Dolores organized a game of duck, duck goose, kids would join in and play and afterward help them pick up trash. Children never asked to participate; they just joined in. John and Dolores learned their names when they heard the other children shout to them. They had foul mouths. If John asked them to be quiet they would tell him to fuck off. They feared nothing. John and Dolores could scold them all day long, but what was that compared to what they had seen and been through at home? They defended what little they had. If someone stepped on their shoes, that was considered being disrespectful and that can't stand. Like Bigg Man once told him, If you walk through the 'hood with your bling and your grillz you can't let anyone disrespect you.

John and Dolores drew lines: Here's the rule you broke. You're suspended for two days. They suspended kids a lot in the early days. Now, many of the adults who participate in Light of the Village today grew up in the church, so when their children act up they discipline them. That helps—and a dose of humor.

The work, however, can be taxing. John leaves many days wondering: What the heck am I doing? Over the years those feelings of despondency have become less frequent. He and Dolores knew what they were called to do and there was enough progress to keep them at it. They could have moved to another neighborhood, another town. They could easily find verses in the Bible to support such a decision. Throw a few of those out there and leave in good conscience. But they always felt like, no, the Village was it. To say they wanted to practice God's Word but find an easier place to do it felt like hypocrisy. No one said it would be easy. To believe in something is hard. Faith is hard. Their commitment, they believe, shows their devotion to the Village and its people. He and Dolores have each other and their Christian ideals. They vent and carry on. They weren't in the Village every day at first. If they had a bad weekend they might not return for another seven days and avoid being bombarded with need every single day. Now they come to the Village almost daily except Friday and Saturday, but they worked up to that. They've acquired resilience and an ability to reset. They can have a terrible day but the next unfolds as a whole new chapter. The unpredictability comes from what the families they see experience which is much more than anything they've gone through, certainly. So, they don't let their own exhaustion interfere. They remain consistent and genuine to build trust—for them, an investment. They never promise anything they can't deliver, and they try not to disappoint. John and Dolores chose to be in the Village. We love God and love you, John has said from the very beginning in Bible studies but he won't be intimidated. Well, Mr. John, if you don't let me do such and such, I won't come back. OK, John says, we'll miss you. Or a mother will say, If you don't pay my electric bill I won't let my kids come to the church. OK, we'll miss them. Da'Cino's mother pulled that little stunt. She threatened to send him to live with his stepdad Joe in Detroit. She needed $1,150 to pay a utility bill. Da'Cino was seventeen at the time and wouldn't have gone, but still … John has no idea what kind of life Da'Cino's mother has lived to make her think she can use her son as leverage. A life of desperation, he assumes, but it still angers him.

He knows what he wants for these families now and what they will want for themselves most likely aren't the same, and he has to let go but can be available to support them while they make their own decisions. John and Dolores got their feelings hurt in the early days hoping for change on terms that made sense to them but over time they realized it wasn't about them. Their years in the Village have taught them not to overestimate their influence. Give someone commonsense advice they think will help them but be prepared for them to disregard it. Hey, do you think you should get your driver's license? Do you want me to take you? No, and then they get angry because you didn't take them. John doesn't pretend to understand. It's complex. He and Dolores don't get their feelings hurt now. They've hardened. They keep their hopes and expectations to a minimum.

On a Tuesday evening, John picks up children for the ministry's after-school program. They'll play games and have about a half hour of Bible study. He drives beneath the Interstate 65 overpass into a neighborhood of small brick houses with peeling white trim. Bare bulbs cast a pale yellow light over empty porches. He turns into a housing project, parks outside a home, and beeps.

Here's Yolanda, Courtney, and Shalanda, he shouts at three girls hurrying toward the van, backpacks bouncing. What's up, Bo?

What's up, Bo? they shout back to him.

What're you drinking, Bo?

Orange juice, Yolanda says.

A little OJ. What you up to, Shalanda?

Watching YouTube cartoons.

They clamber into the van. Shalanda finds a Ziplock bag with half a sandwich.

There's food back here.

We'll throw it away, John says. I tried to clean it up for y'all. What kind of food?

It's a mushed something. It stinks.

We'll throw it away. Where's your grandmother?

She's not coming today. Not feeling well.

She OK?

She's OK.

Let's roll.

John starts driving.

We have to pick up Jerome and a few others. What do you think? he asks.

Good.

OK. That's a good attitude.

Mr. John?

Yeah, Bo?

Rosa Parks didn't want to move on the bus, Shalanda says. We learned about her in class today. Was she and Martin Luther King friends?

No, Courtney answers.

Yes, Yolanda counters.

They were partners in the fight for civil rights, for sure, John says.

Rosa Parks was sitting down and a white person wanted her seat and Rosa Parks said, No, I'm not going to move out of my seat, Shalanda says. You better go back there, white person, because I was here first, and that is right because she was there first.

Corey "Bigg Mann" Davis with John and Dolores Eads, January 2021.

Miz Julia Gordon

Paul McGuire

Betty Catlin

Aaron "Billy Boy" Amison sitting on an abandoned tub, Alabama Village.

Patricia "Pony" Hayward with her son, Cordell.

Cindy Darrington

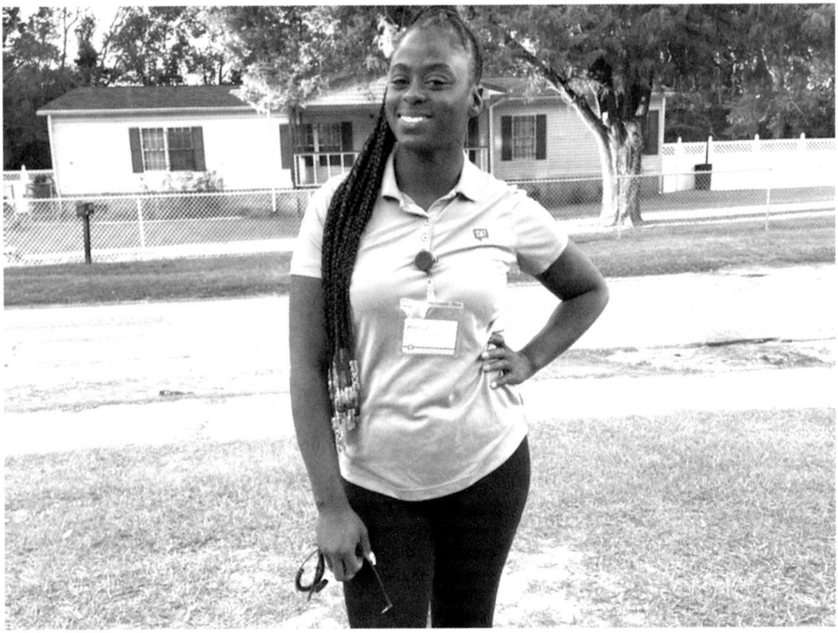

Jesenda Brown

Tommie Bonner

Light of the Village playground

Da'Cino Dees

Hood Child insignia on a sweatshirt.

Marion "Mayo" Awudu

Lawrence "LRG" Davis

Arthur Williams

Daniel "Dee Tee" Tillman

Jamez Montgomery in the stocking cap in Bible study at the church

Memorial Wall

That's true, John says.

And then white people got angry and she got arrested.

Hank Aaron, we read about him too, Courtney says.

He grew up in Mobile, John says. He's from Toulminville.

He played baseball.

He was good. He had made a lot of inroads. Progress, let's call it progress, John says. Like Rosa Parks, he had to take a stand to make things for the better. You guys learned a lot.

I learned about math and science, Yolanda says.

Sounds like you guys did pretty good today.

I got all B's, Shalanda says.

I got all A's, Yolanda says.

John stops at a squat house surrounded by trees.

Hey, Bo! John shouts to a boy running toward him.

—◦∿◦—

Young men who participated in the after-school program as children often visit with John and Dolores, especially after a shooting. Bigg Man came by once with bullet holes in his car. He wanted them to know he had survived a shootout.

On this evening, twenty-eight-year-old Daniel "Dee Tee" Tillman stops at the church. He wears a T-shirt and windbreaker and dark blue jeans. He pushes his sunglasses up in his hair. John stands outside and watches the few cars driving past.

What up, Bo?

Awright, Mr. John.

Dee Tee used to belong to the Yard Dogs, an association he still speaks of with pride. The Yard Dogs were older and

John and Dolores kept them separated from the younger boys concerned about their being a bad influence. At the same time, they wanted to involve them in some way so they didn't feel rejected. Work was the answer. John would pay them to mow grass and pick up trash. A staff member, Ken, collected the names of Village families who wanted their yards cut. He would then take the boys, usually ten to twelve of them, out in his truck to do the work. The boys loved getting paid ten dollars apiece every week. They earned money and had something to do and remained part of the church. Dee Tee remembers how Bigg Man kept the water jugs filled.

Shootings and the delinquent behavior of some of the boys discouraged Ken, and he eventually grew so disheartened he quit. The Yard Dogs too, became less enthusiastic. Cutting lawns for ten dollars a week lost its attraction the older they became. The group disbanded, lured by more lucrative street opportunities.

Dee Tee pulls up his left pants leg and shows John a scar from a bullet wound that resembles a cobweb. He was messing with this girl and her boyfriend shot him. Homeboy didn't understand. She was just Dee Tee's homegirl, nothing more, but homeboy got to tripping and shot him.

See how my good leg moves around? Dee Tee says. I can't do that with my hurt leg. I can't bend it.

John shakes his head.

You need help with seeing a doctor? You need a specialist, Bo?

No, I'm good, Mr. John, thank you.

What did it feel like?

Getting shot? When it happens, you don't feel it at first when your adrenaline is going. Soon as you realize you're shot it just burns, man, and your whole body starts sweating. You want water, immediately, man. You know how it is if you eat some bad food and you start sweating and you got a messed-up stomach? That's how it feels. Then the pain comes after that. You don't care about warrants or nothing. Worry about that later; just get me to a doctor.

You don't have any pain or whatever in your leg now?

Sometimes.

Like where?

Like in my knee. It don't lock in. I can't straighten it all the way. I can't hold it straight out all the way, either.

If it gets cold or rains, does that mess it up more?

Some.

Let us know if you need anything.

I will.

John checks out Dee Tee's pants.

Nice blue jeans, Bo. New?

These jeans right here? What I got on?

Yeah, a little tight, Bo. Are you making a fashion statement?

You know they're just straight and tight.

Does that help your leg?

A little.

Dee Tee looks around. The pitch dark cloaks most everything beyond the lights of the church. He recalls every time some-body moved out of the Village, scavengers tore up the empty house to steal the copper wiring. Then the owner or landlord would burn it down for the insurance money. Nobody could move in to nothing, so lot after lot turned into a pile of ashes overgrown by weeds, until the Village looked like it does today. Dee Tee set a couple of houses on fire for fun, he ain't going to lie. High and drunk, chilling, and he just set this little vacant house on fire and the next thing he and his homeboys knew, it set to blazing. They ran out to the street and watched it burn.

A drug bust landed Dee Tee in jail recently. He called Mr. John every day and he always picked up. Dee Tee got out on his own recognizance and is selling pot again, still being bad, he admits. But when he's at the church, he's at the church and behaves. He's a good fella when he needs to be.

You are, John says.

I just have my shyster ways.

Is that what you call it?

Dee Tee laughs. Life man, it just drags him down. He gets a phone call from one of his homeboys: Hey, Dee Tee, this, this, and this is going down. I need you. How can he turn down someone who never refused him in a time of need? How can he say, No, I ain't with it? That would be like ignoring his momma when she done took care of him his whole life. In the streets, he can't turn the other cheek. No one can. He can walk away but for how long? How long can he avoid trouble? Will he run for the rest of his life or will he protect himself and his homeboys? Some asshole might not like him for something his big brother did or because of where he lives. Does that mean he has to avoid them every day? He won't let anyone kill him or his friends and family. He will fight. Not because he wants to, but because he won't be taunted or beaten up or shot.

There're always alternatives, John says.

Not for me.

You have options, Bo.

I know. I take them when I can.

Doesn't seem like it. Your back hurt? You were shot there too, right?

Yeah, Dee Tee says, but it don't never hurt.

That's crazy. Your leg hurts but not your back.

You know the bullet in my back moved around to my stomach. Doctors got it out with something they put in my butt.

How'd that feel? I hope you were knocked out.

Oh, yeah. They stuck a video camera down my throat and stuck me up my other end too.

Did you feel violated?

Dee Tee laughs.

A little.

He plays a recording on his phone: "I'm shot, Smoke! [*Gasping.*] I'm shot."

That's me. Hear how I'm breathing? Fast right?

You recorded yourself? John says.

I thought I was going to die. I called my homeboy. I wanted him to know what happened.

That's crazy, Bo.

John takes out his phone and shows Dee Tee a photo of a bullet.

You know Baby C?

Pony's brother?

Right. He got shot in the butt. About three weeks later the bullet came out in church like a splinter.

Dee Tee looks at the photo,

Ah, he must've been a proud father.

I had to pull it out, John says.

You did?

I wore gloves.

Good.

It had mostly come out.

Sticking out?

Yes.

Sometimes doctors leave the bullet in, Dee Tee says. They tell you it's just going to come out by itself. You know your body just going to push it out. Anything that don't supposed to be in your body, your body going to push it out. I promise you that, for real.

John pockets his phone. Dee Tee stares across the street. He feels calm and in no hurry to leave or for further conversation. He considers the church a haven, a kind of demilitarized zone. Don't nothing bad go on here. No matter what happens beyond this little circle where he and Mr. John stand, ain't nothing bad going on inside the circle. No shooting, no cussing, nothing like that. Can't no one come up here with any mess. When Dee Tee and his homeboys were younger they would get into it at the church, fighting and stuff, a little bit, but when they got older they understood that Mr. John and Miz Dolores were there for them, and they protected it. Ain't no break-ins here. Nobody stealing the AC unit or busting out windows and setting things on fire. This isn't a place to play like that. This here is the only good spot in the whole Village.

How many times did you have to say something twice to us, Mr. John, when we was little to get us to chill?

Not very often now. But when we first started …

We was bad then wasn't we?

Dolores doesn't have to say anything twice.

She just look at you. For a short woman, she can give you a hard look.

I got pictures of her telling you to put your shirt on and stop smoking.

Remember when we went to that Veteran's Day thing with the big luncheon?

Back in 2006, John says. And the speaker, a general or something asked, How many of y'all have been shot at? And he meant shot at in a war. He was trying to make a point about combat. Well, our whole table stood up.

Dee Tee starts laughing.

Everybody been shot at, he says.

And they said no, no, not that kind, John says. And y'all said, Well, we've been shot at.

And we was like fifteen, sixteen. Bigg Man, all of us. We were caught up in the life, Mr. John. Still are. It's either, or. It's going to be him, or it's going to be me. It's just going to be like that. We just out there having to throw down and deal with it. When you go in the house, who's to say no one's going to come and kick in your front door? Who's to say they ain't sitting outside ready to shoot up your crib? As long as I make it through the night, I'm going to see another day. But I don't worry when I'm here.

You always have options, Bo.

Ain't no one looking out for us in the streets, Mr. John.

Ain't no one saying, Shoot back, either.

Dee Tee kicks at the ground. Rolls a pebble beneath his right foot.

It's been a minute since I seen you, Mr. John.

It has. You're welcome here any time, Bo. You know that.

I got to head on.

I know.

He watches Dee Tee drive off. What can he do with someone like that? The street, he thinks, is addictive as any drug. Dee Tee could leave it, he could ask John, What can I do with my life? and John would help him figure something out, but he can't force it. He can only ask questions in the hope they will supply the answers. John sees life in the Village as ongoing traumatic stress, not post-traumatic stress. Nothing "post" about it. If he stopped and considered his life, Dee Tee might feel overwhelmed by all that he has seen and done, most of it unpleasant. The street adds to those memories every day, but it also distracts with its drama. John tries to understand the motivation of someone like Dee Tee but he can't, not completely, despite the years he has spent here. He sees no endgame, no triumphant final statistic. He hates hearing so many sad stories. But death hovers here, a presence as tangible as all the ruined houses and as unpredictable as the weather. People die. They get shot. Not all of them but too many at too young an age. Does he not talk about them because they can't be placed in the positive statistic column? Da'Cino is a good story, and Jesenda. She seems to be doing well. Who is John, who is anyone, to suggest that isn't enough? Will they be spared? He doesn't know.

He feels certain there must be a balance between the pulling-yourself-up-by-the-bootstraps crap and giving them everything they ask for, but he hasn't found it yet. Dolores asked him one day, What do you think you'd be doing if you grew up in the Village? He can't answer that. He didn't grow up in the Village. He will never know. As a kid he screwed up, but he held a minimum wage job and put himself through school. It was difficult at times, but he never quit. He came from a single-parent home, but he had some sense even when he behaved like a knucklehead. He had things these kids don't and probably never will. A father who put him in a private military school, for one. He can't force his good fortune on anyone. An older woman once told Dolores how she survived the Depression. If she could do it, she said, the kids in the Village could too. John disagreed. Another load of crap. It's not the same. Not the same type of poverty, and oh, by the way, lady, not everyone survived the Depression either. Just FYI. She was fortunate. Not everyone is. People like to go for the quick answer, and more often than not that proves inaccurate. He can't force anyone to be self-sufficient. He'd like to but he can't. He won't judge. No one should, especially if they haven't been to the Village. They need to get down here and meet these families. Learn to accept that many make bad choices—who doesn't?—and still find it in their hearts to love them. Accept that they may have a positive influence and never know it. Not knowing is hard. Accepting the not-knowing is one form of success.

—⁓—

John walks the perimeter of the ministry, hears the children laughing inside, keeps moving slowly, holding a walkie-talkie to communicate with staff inside. His gaze flits between buildings. His shoes scrape against stones. He never knows who might drop by and what their mood might be, agitated or friendly. He enjoyed seeing Dee Tee but he might not know the next person who stops. Better to assess the situation outside, away from the kids. He compares Light of the Village to a forward operating base. Over the years, he and Dolores have established codes: *Broken arrow* means gunshots in the area, *Mike Tyson* means a fight. Hand signals too: Fingers shaped like a phone receiver means to call 911. The codes resulted from an encounter one afternoon in June 2015 when a man who was convicted of murder and just released from prison drove to the ministry, erroneously believing John and Dolores were holding his daughter.

The man's name was Tyroon. The girl had been adopted after her mother died of a drug overdose while Tyroon was locked up but no one had told him. He rolled up to the ministry with his sister and a friend with her baby. The women had told him his daughter was at the ministry because her mother had used its services. John stood inside with about one hundred children enrolled in summer camp; Dolores was outside. Tyroon got out of the car, walked toward her and pointed a finger.

Where's my daughter? he shouted.

I don't know where she is, Dolores said, trying to stay calm, but her heart hammered against her chest. She worried he might hit her. He continued shouting, shaking like he would burst through his skin. John heard the commotion and hurried outside. Tyroon turned and faced him.

I want my child! he demanded.

John raised his hands, a signal for calm.

We don't know where she is, dude.

I want my fucking child!

Man, you got to chill out.

John had a crazy kind of wish for Tyroon to clock him with a solid right hook and end this. Instead, Tyroon stormed back to his car and opened the back door. John followed. He saw Tyroon reach for a revolver. John had few options, none of them good: to fight but with two women and a child in the car, that wouldn't end well; to run but that would put himself and the children inside at risk if Tyroon started shooting; or to keep talking.

Dude, we don't have your daughter.

A woman named Tyra Quinie, who had been studying for her GED rushed outside and started shouting at Tyroon. He cussed her out and leaned into the car for the gun. John glanced at Dolores and their eyes locked and he gave her a well-this-is-it kind of look. The thought comforted him. He stood in the presence of God, his wife, and the ministry— everything he had devoted his life to. Whatever happened, he belonged here.

We're going to get through this, Dolores told herself. It will be OK, but she knew it might not be. It will be OK, she told herself again. She dialed 911. When she got off the phone, she shouted, The police are on the way!

Tyroon jumped in the car and slammed the door. He cussed out John and sped off just as the children wandered outside. Unaware of what had happened, they began playing. John watched them. He felt OK. He hadn't panicked, had stayed focused. Some volunteers, however, left and didn't return.

Later that afternoon, a brother of Tyroon's called John and put him on the phone. He apologized. The two women, he said, had told him John had his baby.

OK, John said, let me stop you right there. The police are looking for you. You're out on parole for murder. Chill out, go to the police, and we'll come by and see you.

Tyroon turned himself in. When John and Dolores arrived at the Prichard police station, a detective told them that if they pressed charges Tyroon would probably do fifteen years. He cried and apologized again when they met with him. He had been played by people spreading rumors about his child, he said, and the two women in the car had egged him on. John and Dolores believed him. He had a manila folder with cards from his daughter. He brought it with him because he assumed he was going back to prison.

No, dude it's all good, John said. If we can help you get a job, whatever, come by and we'll see what we can do.

John and Dolores have seen him twice since then. They said hello, and nothing more. John believes that if someone commits a crime they should be punished. Throw away the key, he gets that. At the same time, they need to be helped when they get released—because they will get out. Tyroon had nothing. His daughter was gone and no one had told him. John and Dolores took the brunt of his anger, understood, and forgave him. Then the three of them moved on.

Tyra Quinie thinks God told her to rush outside when Tyroon pulled up. She hadn't heard a thing, just looked up from her desk and decided to take a look. Because they believed in her, she thought of John and Dolores as her parents. Her real father was mostly absent from her life and her mother was around but stayed to herself because she was deaf. Tyra relied on and trusted Mr. John and Miz Dolores in a way she never could with her parents. When she saw Tyroon yelling at Mr. John, she lost it. Tyroon called her all kinds of names but Tyra didn't care. If you're going to hurt Mr. John, you're going to hurt me first, she yelled.

Tyra had met Mr. John and Miz Dolores years earlier when she worked at a Prichard gym, now closed. Many of the children she supervised participated in the ministry's programs. One day, Tyra dropped by looking for two sisters. Their mother had died of AIDS, and Tyra had not seen them at the gym for a while but she knew they ate breakfast at the ministry. (One of them, Shadarrius, later died from a drug overdose. Her picture hangs on the Memorial Wall.)

The Lord spoke to Tyra as she stopped outside the ministry that day. She knows how that sounds, but she's not asking anyone to believe her. She believes it and that's what matters. Tyra, God told her, I want you to get your GED. She was about twenty-seven and could barely read. Miz Dolores and Mr. John told her, You can get your GED. You can do this. Miz Dolores was adamant: If you don't try, then you don't want it. All you gotta do is try.

Miz Dolores helped Tyra study. She took the GED but failed by eighteen points. However, she aced the reading test. Undeterred, she took it again and passed. Then the Lord told her, I want you to go to college. Tyra told Mr. John, I don't know what it is but the Lord says I should go to college. I guess you're going to college, Mr. John said, and she did. These days, she works at Amazon. She trains and supervises drivers.

Tyra owns a house in Prichard, but when she was younger, she'd lived in the Village when her family moved there from the Orange Grove Projects near downtown Mobile. Orange Grove had its rough edges but it had nothing on the Village. She learned quickly that life was real in the Village, no joke. When Tyra first came to the ministry, the Memorial Wall held only one photo. Now look at it. More photos will go up, she has no doubt, but hers, she prays, won't be one of them. She has all that she needs, not much but enough, and she doesn't mess around. Many families in the Village have much less, and therefore they have nothing to lose. That's one reason for the violence.

Tyra has seen plenty of people shot. She knew Mayo. He was soft on her. He could make her laugh so hard she thought she'd die. Bigg Man was upset when Mayo died. What's going on? he asked Tyra. They done shot Mayo! She can go to Bigg Man for anything just like she could with Mayo. Bigg Man, I need

$120 for my light bill. OK, come and get it. He had a girlfriend who shot him in the butt. Laid up in his bed, he laughed telling Tyra about it.

She saw her best friend shoot another man in front of a convenience store. Nothing she could do but step back, run for cover, mourn the loss, and cry for the ones left behind. Don't be naive, Mr. John taught her, and have faith in God. Sunday is the most important day of the week for Tyra. She attends Bible study and renews her faith. Then she goes home and lives the best life she can. Many people in the Village have repented. They grew up and quit playing. No one knows what path someone will take. The boy with a gun might become the man kneeling in prayer. No one should give up on the Village. Look at her. She learned to read. Who would have thought?

3

A guy named "Yellow" was the first young man John and Dolores knew who died in the Village. Kind of knew. Not well. Shot. The first person they knew well who died was a young man everyone called "Mook." They'd known him since he was a child. When they first came to the Village, they ran into him and other kids. As they talked, it started raining and they all dashed under a porch, gray storm clouds scudding above them. Mook enjoyed showing them around. He had a mild manner then, but he sold drugs. Over the years, he moved deeper into the game, and developed a volatile temper. He died after a former girlfriend told him she was with another man in the Roger Williams Housing Projects in Mobile. Mook drove there and confronted him. They fought to a draw and Mook left. The man got a gun and called Mook and dared him to return. Mook did. The man had locked the front door so Mook pulled the AC unit out of a window and crawled inside and the man shot him.

The violence can take bizarre, darkly humorous twists. Like George and the muffin. Sounds like a children's book, doesn't it? John thinks. George was always out there a little bit, and he had made enemies. One afternoon a sedan drove into a lot next to the ministry, and the two men inside started shooting at George. He ran behind a house holding a muffin. The shooters quickly sped through and out. George peeked from around the house and smiled, showing his gold teeth. He had not dropped his muffin. It was a good muffin, he said. That stuck with people. George and the muffin assumed the status of folklore. A few years later and not long after he had moved to Florida, police found skeletal remains in an abandoned car.

Joseph Torres killed a man at fifteen. He had been involved with the ministry since he was a child. His mother died of cancer when he was young and he lived with an aunt. Like Mook, his moods ran hot and cold. If Joseph liked someone, he liked them 100 percent and would do anything for them. But if he disliked someone, he ignored them; they didn't exist. He knew how to take charge. If he saw kids fighting, he'd stop it through his presence, by the way he carried himself, without speaking a word.

One December night in 2008, days before Christmas, Joseph and his friend, Johiterio, Miz Betty's son, stopped at the ministry and said they wanted to go beyond their church group and become professional rappers. Joseph asked for money to buy shoes but John and Dolores didn't have enough and the boys got angry.

We're going to go make music, they said, and stalked off. John and Dolores didn't hear from Joseph again until April 25, 2009, a Saturday night, when he shot forty-two-year-old Benjamin Henry on D block. Benjamin didn't live in the Village but he knew people there and stayed on Baldwin from time to time. He stopped at the church for a barbecue one afternoon but John and Dolores didn't know him well. He was tall and lean with a trim mustache. He wore button-down shirts and blue jeans. He drove a Cadillac Coupe DeVille or something similar and enjoyed working on cars just down the road from the church and not too far from the hit house.

Joseph, Johiterio, and a third teenager, Antonio Hall, whom John and Dolores had never met assumed Benjamin had money and decided to rob him. As he sat in his car, Joseph approached the driver's side carrying a sawed-off shotgun. At some point in their confrontation he blew a hole in Benjamin's chest. He, Johiterio, and Antonio fled. Joseph would later claim the gun had misfired.

John heard about the shooting the next day, a Sunday morning. He was preparing a Bible lesson at home when his phone rang. A couple in the Village who volunteered at the church was on the other end. Two of your boys killed a guy, they said, Joseph and Johiterio. *Two of your boys,* John repeated to himself as if it was his fault. OK, whatever.

Dolores couldn't believe it. She would not have been surprised if Joseph had been stopped for selling weed, but murder? What happened? she wondered. What went wrong? What had they missed? Joseph did chores around the church and he would help children read the Psalms in Bible study. He kept the building clean without anyone asking but there was another side to him. If he didn't get what he wanted, he would throw tantrums. When he was twelve years old he told other boys at the church not to talk to Dolores because she had upset him, and they obeyed him until he settled down. Kids followed Joseph. He had charisma and a big ego. He saw dollar signs with his rapping. He was slim but stocky. He kept his hair short. He smiled easily but he could be menacing when he became angry.

She took him and other boys on a field trip to Dauphin Beach one year. The low water allowed her, Joseph, and Bigg Man's little brother, Kirk-Kirk, to walk out on a sandbar and into the water beyond it. They laughed and splashed each other until Dolores noticed Da'Cino and Johiterio on the beach screaming and pointing. She turned around and saw an eight-foot shark swimming toward the sandbar. They started running toward the shore. C'mon! Joseph shouted but Dolores kept falling. Joseph grabbed her and Kirk-Kirk and pulled them with him to safety. Still it was scary.

Now that boy who helped her run from a shark had killed a man.

John and Dolores hurried out of their house and drove to the church. Children and their mothers had already begun gathering in anticipation of the morning's service. Dolores stayed with them while John walked to D block with Da'Cino. It was a little before eight o'clock, a clear, warm day. Yellow police tape cordoned off the street. A crowd including Bigg Man and Mayo lingered. They and everyone else said Joseph had done it. As John and Da'Cino walked back to Light of the Village, Joseph called.

Hey, Mr. John, we need to talk.

They agreed to meet at the church. Joseph showed up about an hour and a half later. Dolores took care of Bible study while John took him into the food closet, the only private place to talk. Joseph sat on a cooler; John stood beside him by a shelf stocked with canned chicken noodle soup.

First off, how are you doing? John asked him.

I screwed up, Joseph said.

John nodded. He said a prayer for peace and guidance. When he finished Joseph admitted he'd killed Benjamin.

I shot him, he said.

John didn't quite know what to say to that, although he knew it to be true.

Let's come up with a plan, he said. What would God want you to do?

I think I need to turn myself in, Joseph said.

You know what that means?

I do.

Joseph wasn't scared. He had never been one to show fear. What remorse he felt he kept to himself. He seemed more upset that he had ruined his future. Like the menu of his life had just been shredded.

You want to turn yourself in now?

Yes. They'll put it on someone else, and I did it.

If you're going to turn yourself in, we don't want it to go badly. The police are probably amped up because they think you're armed and dangerous and all that.

John suggested they call his family. He didn't want them to think he had forced Joseph to turn himself in which could create problems later on if the family blamed him for Joseph being in jail.

I'm going to turn myself in, Joseph told his sister Shay.

John asked if he wanted him or his family to drive him to the Prichard police station. Joseph covered the phone.

I want you to take me, he said.

Probably because almost everyone in his family has warrants, John thought.

OK, I'll do it, he said.

Another sister, Jessica, told Joseph they would meet him at the station.

After Joseph hung up, John called the police.

A young man who was involved in the murder in Alabama Village last night wants to turn himself in, he said. How do we do that?

The dispatcher transferred him to a detective.

He can come to the station, the detective said.

I can bring him, John said.

As they left the church, Dolores walked up to Joseph. She had always wanted children but she suffered from extreme endometriosis, a disease in which tissue similar to the lining of the uterus grows outside of it. At thirty-two, she had a hysterectomy. She had hoped that the children at the church would accept her as a sort of mother figure. Now she knew that had been a false hope. Neither Joseph nor any of the other kids could be her children. She could guide and nurture them, but she could not parent them. They had mothers of their own and had been raised in an environment with pressures and values beyond her influence. That was not her role, she realized as she hugged Joseph, no matter how much she cared for them.

The police station stood behind city hall. John pulled into the parking lot and saw Joseph's family in a car behind a tree. Joseph walked over and embraced each of them. He lingered for a moment before he returned to John and said, Let's do it.

A detective led them into a conference room with a table and chairs and a one-way mirror and did not handcuff Joseph.

Do you want him to stay? the detective asked Joseph, indicating John.

Yes.

The detective turned on a video camera.

Joseph spelled his name. He then gave a statement admitting he had shot Benjamin. He and the two other defendants were charged as adults.

—w—

In December 2010, a judge sentenced Joseph and Antonio to twenty-five years in prison. Bigg Man had given the police a statement and was supposed to testify but he refused to speak when the prosecutor called him. After the sentence, Joseph broke down and apologized to Benjamin's family and his own. Johiterio, who had been on his cell phone when the shooting occurred, received three years but soon after his release police arrested him again for selling drugs and he returned to prison: this time with a twenty-five year stint.

John keeps in touch with Joseph. They talk by phone most Sunday mornings.

What's going on, Bo? You're still in Easterling [Correctional Facility]? You know it's been crazy down here. There's been shootings all over the place. You heard about that? Going back and forth right now. Hopefully things will tamp down a little bit, but yeah it's been kind of nuts. Going on for a little bit. How's COVID? Gone through the place or no? No, that's cool. Hope it all goes away so we can get back to normal. I'm glad you called. We have to work out a visit. We'll try to work that out. It's pretty up there. I know to you it looks the same but we like it. We can travel up there. OK, I'll let you go. We love you, Bo. Holler at you.

———

Joseph tells John he knows he committed a crime. He can only learn from his mistakes and improve his character. It's hard in prison. Step on someone's foot and he may want to fight you. Defend yourself and whoop him, he may want to kill you. A man can go out into the wild like Tarzan and learn to adapt. Prison is no different. He does what it takes to survive. He has changed. He found an older set of dudes behind the walls who took a liking to him and kept him in programs, made him go to classes. He's not fifteen anymore. He resents being defined by a bad decision. It was bad, but what about the good he did? What about all the kids he helped at the church? What about a family he helped move out of the Village? What about saving Miz Dolores and Kirk-Kirk from the shark? None of that gets mentioned.

———

John understands people may wonder how he can say, I love you, Bo, to a murderer. Some people didn't hesitate to criticize Light of the Village on social media.

Wat kind of fake ass church would allow a killa 2 B there! one post read.

We cumin up to that church and find that n-gga! declared another.

Considering the young man he knew, John might easily conclude, Wow, Joseph shouldn't be in prison, but then during the trial the prosecutor showed autopsy photos of Benjamin with a hole in his chest and his mother left the courtroom because she couldn't look at them. John drove to her house in Toulminville, less than four minutes from Prichard, and offered his condolences. One of Benjamin's sisters accepted a fruit basket from him. Thanked him but said nothing more.

Benjamin had a life. John makes no excuses for Joseph. Punish him, yes, he has no problem with that, but he sees no downside to showing him love. He doesn't know a perfect person, however that would be defined. There needs to be a process in place when the time comes for them to walk out, because in twenty-five years Joseph will be released, at some point he will have served his sentence. There has to be something for him here.

What would Jesus do? John hates that cliché but he can't help but ask the question. What would he do? As John sees it, life isn't about second chances. It's about chance after chance after chance. Only death closes the door.

4

Miz Betty talks to Johiterio, every other day. She sends money to his prison account. One day at a time, prayer and faith, Betty reminds herself.

"Lil OG" Catlin, Miz Betty's youngest son, raps about the streets, about fast money and the temptations that brought down his brother Johiterio and Joseph. How they all came from the Village. Everybody going through the struggle. His own with multiple sclerosis. It don't stop him. Only thirty years old, but nothing he can do about it. He lives with his momma and spends most of his time in his bedroom. Bent over his phone, his braided hair falls along both sides of his face, and when he speaks, a flicker of gold reveals itself in his front teeth.

OG learned to do without as a child. He watched his momma fall behind on bills, lights and water cut off. One-parent household, one paycheck. Couldn't go outside for all the shootings. It wasn't as bad as it is today. Now there's zero understanding on the streets. He doesn't like to talk about it for real. The Village could be righteous, it could be fun. Playing football, normal 'hood, for real. People out talking, drinking but the older everyone got, the crazier they got. It's in them. That's how Johiterio and Joseph got in trouble. That's why Da'Cino—that's OG's dawg right there—can't leave. He wants to, but he can't. Shit, it's in him. But everyone wants to go. No one wants to stay. Save up enough money to move up out of there. OG's momma did but that was a rare thing. Get out, see the world, shit. Here, he doesn't even leave his room unless he goes to a studio. Otherwise, he stays in the crib, and chills

His homeboy had a rap video shoot in Atlanta recently and OG said, Fuck it, and went along and ended up recording a song. He worked fast, Atlanta's studios are expensive, like eighty dollars an hour. He did his song in twenty minutes. He's been rapping for so long it's easy for him. Freestyling, cutting loose with whatever words enter his mind. Always about the struggle for real and everything that goes on in the Village. All his lost homeboys. In Prichard, even in Mobile, no one knows what to expect. He riffs on what he feels. Every day is a risk. The streets are dangerous. A lot of situations, for real, go down. He has never been in an altercation or cross-fire situation, yeah, for real, for real, but when he hears of a shooting he thinks, Damn that could've been me. He has felt that way many times.

He was probably twelve, thirteen when he started rapping. It was just something to do. Back then, you had to know how to rap. Now, everybody is just talking and calling it rap. He raps on street shit. Others rap it but can't vouch for it. They didn't live it. His shit is for real about what's going on in Alabama Village. He ain't doing no fairy-tale shit.

He ain't no kid no more. He ain't into all what Dee Tee is about, I gotta go right now, my homeboy needs me, you with me? Does Dee Tee or whoever want to live? That's what he needs to think about. Johiterio and Joseph too. When your partner calls, you might be with your people having family time, for real. That one phone call can take you out when all you had to do was say, No, But you said, OK yeah, I be on my way, and you don't make it back home, and your family's without you. Shit. When all you had to say was, I'm tending to my business, leave me alone. OG doesn't even ride with folks now. Homeboys stop and see him. The same thing they do in a car they can do in his crib. Smoke weed, whatever, watch TV. All that joyriding and shit is over with. OG wants to live.He started a clothing line, Hood Child, to feed off his rap themes. The Hood Child logo shows a man in a hoodie flipping the bird and holding a gun with a blunt hanging out of his mouth. A homeboy drew it. OG liked it and thought, Why not put that on some clothes? He always liked to dress up. He got on his computer, looked up shirts, hoodies and sweatpants, and found a vendor in Pakistan. He sent them the logo and they did a mock-up on different colored T-shirts. OG ordered one hundred and they sold fast.

Stacks of Hood Child T-shirts line the walls of his bedroom. A rack of shelves holds more. Customers order online, business is growing. He wants to expand his inventory, get bigger, rent a storefront. Got sweatpants on the way. He thinks Hood Child remains popular because the logo speaks the truth about the streets. You got guns, you got people that do drugs, shoot dice, people who like to flex their money. Those are the people of the 'hood. Each one of them is a 'hood child. Maybe someone will invest when they see how well his clothes sell.

OG FaceTimes his man in Pakistan and though he doesn't understand him sometimes because of the accent, they do alright and he places orders through MoneyGram. If he pays thirty dollars for a pair of sweatshirts and sweatpants, he'll charge his customers eighty or eighty-five dollars. Reasonable price, good profit. He posts pictures of mock-ups and orders the clothes that receive the most likes. Oh y'all dig this? Y'all like what I got going on with this shirt or these pants? You feelin' this set? Cool, and he places an order and sells it online. Gets his momma to ship them out, or people come to him.

He'd like to bump heads with folks who know more about marketing than he does. People who can help a brother instead of watching him and sitting back and thinking, Look at his stupid ass. He should be doing this, this, and this.

OG plans to make other logos without the gun, the middle finger, and the blunt so kids can wear them to school. It's a good day when people order Hood Child T-shirts for parties. A good day means that on other slow days he can hang and chill because he has money. Take a break. When people want more clothes, they'll hit him up.

He wants to combine his rapping with his clothing line somehow. Move to Atlanta or Dallas, for real. Record and rent a storefront for Hood Child. He wants to escape the streets, but he can't. Without the streets he wouldn't be rapping and there'd be no Hood Child. It would've been best if he had found another route and avoided that mess but the streets are in him, just as they are for Johiterio and Joseph and everyone he knows.

5

Da'Cino doesn't get how Miz Betty keeps it together with a child in prison. She goes out and has her little alone time, he supposes. She and his momma used to kick it together. Best friends. He was always at Miz Betty's house. He knows OG, has a Hood Child windbreaker. OG plays it down but he's big with clothes. Because he has multiple sclerosis, he can't be in the streets but he knows them. Everyone he hangs with lives in the 'hood. His songs aren't bad. His stuff now is way better than his older stuff. He connected with this one dude who used to stop at the church. He sold Beats and hooked up with OG, and now he sounds much better. He promotes his music on YouTube. He uses the profits from Hood Child to pay for his studio time.

Everyone knows not to mess with him because once Johiterio gets out of prison, he would tear their asses up.

Da'Cino always liked Joseph Torres, thought he was pretty cool. Meet him on the street and no one would think he'd kill nobody, but if he got angry, hell yeah he would. He has a quiet, I'm-going-to-get-you kind of temper. If he didn't get you back that day, he'd mess with you on other days. People knew him as a fighter. He and Billy Boy are cousins. Every man in their family has been in jail except for a younger brother. His uncle Rodney got shot in the right leg and can't bend it. Used to play basketball with his leg out all stiff.

Da'Cino looks at it like this: Moms lose control of their kids and give up and the kids live in the street and hang out with older people who have been in the street for years. The streets are a rush. There's nothing to do, but there's always something to do. Even if it's not good, you can always find a way to get your heart pumping, and someone will be out there to draw you in deeper. The fast money allows you to get whatever you want and you don't need your mommas anymore. Mommas say, Stay inside, and the kid says, Hey, I got to go and make my money.

That's Bigg Man. He doesn't want to work because he wants that fast money. Da'Cino gets it but he has no desire to get shot or be in prison. He doesn't want to deal with the consequences that come with fast money—that's his thing. Bigg Man never talks about getting hurt. He feels everybody knows him, whatever. He doesn't have enemies Da'Cino knows of, but he does carry a pistol in his glove compartment. Bigg Man posted on Facebook, *We are always screaming, Black lives matter, but we're killing each other.*

He's a funny dude. When he relaxes and can be himself, he makes Da'Cino laugh. Goofy kind of humor. One time, some Village girls got into a beef with girls from outside the 'hood. They all started fighting and Bigg Man took out his phone and started recording it. Then he pepper-sprayed them and said, Y'all get out of here, and they were coughing and he was laughing and spraying them. He thought it was so funny. He can get away with stuff like that because he's Bigg Man.

One Christmas, Bigg Man bought a bunch of bicycles and he organized the crackheads in the Village to put them together. He got on Facebook and said, Y'all want these bikes? Come and get them, man. I got a lot of them. Bring all your kids. And he gave them out. Da'Cino was like, OK, at least he's being nice with his drug money. He's helping people.

He probably got that way from being around Mr. John and Miz Dolores. He wants them to be proud of him. John is the closest thing Bigg Man has to a father. Da'Cino too. John has taught Da'Cino so much. Little things, but important to him. He had never been to a restaurant before John and Dolores took him. He was shocked when he saw teenagers had credit cards and even their own cars. Before he owned his own ride, Da'Cino walked everywhere including downtown Prichard, but it was just Prichard. Wasn't much of a downtown. There were more stores then than now but it was always run-down. Downtown Mobile was *downtown.* The first time he and his brothers went out to eat with John and Dolores, his brothers started clapping at the waiters for their attention. John talked them through the menu and explained how to order. It was a novelty to sit down, eat, and talk.

Da'Cino enjoyed Big Time Diner in Mobile. He always asked to eat there when John and Dolores took him out for his birthday. California Dreaming was another good place. People really stared at him. He was a little Black kid with John and Dolores. He supposes they wondered, What's up with that?

Before Da'Cino met John, he didn't know a place like Big Time Diner or California Dreaming existed. His family drove to Wendy's to eat out. He especially enjoyed the triple hamburger special. When his momma received her income tax refund check, she would give him a little bit of money and he and his brothers would head off to Wendy's. They didn't sit inside and eat. Nothing like that. Never.

Da'Cino had never entered a movie theater, had never seen a big screen until John and Dolores took him. He was eight years old and remembers getting a snack pack: popcorn, candy, and a drink. He thought: What could be more wonderful than sitting in a movie theater eating candy and sucking down a drink? At home he ate what food he could find, and if it was gone by the time he showed up he went hungry. He had to share everything his whole life, but that day at the theater, man, he had his little bit of popcorn, candy, and a drink all to himself. It wasn't that much, but it was his. He can't describe how that felt. To eat his own stuff. Like the world held possibilities he had never dreamed of.

John and Dolores helped him get the job at the Spanish Fort movie theater. He applied and followed up three times, but nothing happened. He asked about his application one day when John and Dolores were with him. These your people? the lady asked. Yes, Da'Cino said. He started work the following week.

He was sixteen then, tall and he supposes intimidating. He didn't smile. He felt people talked about him, the clothes he wore. He didn't have the best. His shirts and pants were either too big or too small. At the start of each school year, it seemed every kid had new clothes but him at the start of each school year. He and his brothers put fresh starch in their hand-me-downs. If they sprayed enough starch and ironed really well they could make a crease look new. Man, Da'Cino ironed the shit out of his pants. He'd be in his room for hours pressing his pants. He'd put them under his mattress so they wouldn't wrinkle. In the morning, he'd iron them again to have that crease but all his friends could still tell they were old clothes.

He remembers the first time he heard John cuss. Dolores cussed the same day. They had just bought him a cell phone. He was at the church and some girls showed up to fight. I don't know how to stop this, Da'Cino thought. He called John: Hey, Kathy and them are getting ready to get into it and I'm the only one here. Shit, John said. Da'Cino started laughing. Then he called Dolores and told her about the girls. Shit, Dolores said, I'm on my way. Da'Cino couldn't stop laughing.

When John and Dolores joke around with someone, that means they love them. John wouldn't tease just anybody the way he pokes fun at Da'Cino. They might think he was disrespecting them and that would cause all sorts of problems. John is the boss but he doesn't throw his power around. Sometimes Da'Cino talks to volunteers and they think he runs the church. White volunteers, college kids, ask him if they can do this and that. He tells them, Man, I don't know, ask John.

As much as he enjoys the church, Da'Cino has thought more and more about leaving. However, he doesn't want to hurt John and Dolores. It's not about them but living in the Lighthouse and all the people who come knocking on his door when the church is closed. He figures it's just time to go. Not in a bad way. He has been at church his whole life. All he knows is the Village and the church. When he worked at the casino, he met new people every day. Here he knows everyone from way back. Nothing new about them or their needs. He feels stuck. When he's at work, he's in the Village, after work he's in the Village. He wonders if he can really leave, though. His momma would still call him for cigarettes and liquor. That would stress him, but if he lived somewhere else he would be away from all her mess. He felt calm when he lived in Spanish Fort. Everything was so close to his apartment. Grocery store right there. The police often stopped him walking to work and checked his book bag. He had nothing in it but the shoes he put on at work but he always wore a black hoodie and that might have bothered them. He just liked hoodies. He had a bunch. The police told him they were investigating break-ins. Da'Cino called John. Do what they ask and be polite, John advised. After they got used to seeing him, the police left Da'Cino alone.

He enjoys the quiet of the suburbs, as weird as it can be sometimes. It used to make him lonely. Now silence feels more like a companion. He used to tell people, I'll never come back to Prichard but, hey, here he is.

He ain't no dumb dude. He can do most jobs but he doesn't have a high school diploma. He has a work history but no education to support it.

Sometimes he wonders what kind of daddy he would be. A lot better than his stepdad, Joe. That wouldn't take much. Joe would sell Da'Cino's sisters for drug money. They don't behave like anything happened to them, but that's what he did. When they hear news reports about child abuse, they get upset. Then Da'Cino sees how Joe hurt them and how they're still dealing with it.

One of his sisters told his momma, but she put it on them. What are you doing to make Joe want to do that? she asked. Da'Cino noticed it bothered his momma when some of her nieces started talking and hanging out with older boys. It was about that time she stopped eating and had to go to the hospital. Maybe that's why she got sick. Bad memories of her failure as a momma. Maybe she remembered how young she was when she got pregnant. Maybe she wasn't thinking about what Joe did to her kids but what some other man did to her when she was only fifteen. Da'Cino never knew what happened to his sisters until he was older and they told him. He had kind of assumed something wrong was going on, but he and his brothers wanted nothing to do with Joe and stayed out of his business. Hey, you riding with me, Joe would tell one of Da'Cino's sisters, and then they'd leave the house together. He never asked the boys to go with him, not that they would've wanted to. Pisses Da'Cino off how that man messed with his family, and his momma said nothing. He would have killed him had he done that to his child.

Da'Cino was on the verge of being a father in 2012. His girlfriend at the time gave birth to his son, Da'Cino Jr., but he died. Da'Cino was twenty-one, young and dumb, in the moment, and then just like that she became pregnant. He vowed that unlike his daddy and stepdaddy, he would be there for his child.

A week before the baby was due, his girlfriend traveled to Jacksonville, Florida, to visit family. She called Da'Cino one afternoon and told him she had passed out and had been rushed to a hospital. The doctor told her the baby had a faint heartbeat. What do we need to do? Da'Cino asked. I need to stay in bed and chill, she told him. The next day, Da'Cino Jr. was stillborn. Da'Cino didn't know what that meant until he asked one of his sisters and she told him.

Da'Cino took the death hard. Angry at the world, he didn't want to talk to anyone, including his girlfriend. The baby was so small. Had he lived, Da'Cino probably wouldn't be working for the ministry because he'd require a bigger salary to support a family. His child would need attention, and he wouldn't have time for ministry kids. Tragedy happens for a reason, he decided. It took him a long time to reach that conclusion and even longer to accept it.

Bigg Man and many of Da'Cino's other homeboys have kids. They speak to their children but they don't take them out or live with their mommas. They'll say, These are my kids, and that's it. Da'Cino doesn't think having a child has anything to do with status. If they can sleep with a girl they will, and if she gets pregnant, oh well. It's not about the number of kids who are born but the number of girls they sleep with. Some dudes call it the body count. That's status. They live for the moment because life can be that short.

Da'Cino remembers Pony carrying Natalia in one arm, her schoolbooks in the other. A kid with a kid. That's how she used to walk everywhere. He helped her get a job at Premiere 14, but the boss man fired her. Her cash drawer kept coming up short. Da'Cino won't say she was stealing. A short drawer speaks for itself.

He sees his sisters with all their kids, how they can get stressed running them around, and he thinks, I don't need to take that on. He has his hands full at the ministry. The kids at the church, man, they can be so bad. He's OK giving them back to their mommas. But he would've loved his son. He carries his photo on his phone, Da'Cino Jr. swaddled in white cloth, eyes closed. The boy's momma recently married. Da'Cino talks to her from time to time. He's happy for her.

He stays on his nieces and nephews: Don't have kids, finish school, find jobs. He knows. He doesn't have a GED. He studied for it and took the test but didn't pass by two lousy points. He should take it again but the thought exhausts him. He studied so hard. If he didn't pass the first time why would the second time be any different? He understands all too well the difficulty of finding work without a high school degree. After he got laid off and despite his experience at the casino and the movie theater, no employer but the church offered to hire him.

—⁓—

Da'Cino gets in his car and cruises, no destination in mind, just driving. The walls close in sometimes being alone in the Lighthouse. Besides, someone will come knocking if he stays.

He sees Tony's Car Wash on Dunlap and Wilson. Tony used to drink. He'd have a beer in his hands 24/7. Morning, noon, and night he was full. In 2008, he told John and Dolores, I got to kick this life. The next day, they put him on a bus to Victory Gospel Chapel. He stayed there ninety days and renewed his faith in God. Now, he has his own business. Twenty dollars a car, no charge for vacuuming.

Da'Cino notices a new Popeyes on Wilson. And a new car wash. Wasn't there the other day. He rolls through downtown. Darkened storefronts, the moody glow of streetlights. Linnie's Hair Design. Lighthouse Academy childcare near the Prichard Mall. Custom Cuts. Trash rolls through an empty lot. A closed pawnshop, shedding its white paint and the lettering that once spelled out its name. Barred windows, dusty shelves. Desks and chairs piled up in twisted columns. *We buy gold*, reads a crooked sign. Cashed checks too, at one time.

Knight's Barber Shop shuttered. Inside, the ceiling and walls collapsing. A warped metal security gate. Another pawnshop: *Car titles, we buy broken jewelry, check cashing*. Exposed pink insulation in the ravaged ceiling. Lotus Club. Opens at 9 p.m. Ten-dollar cover before 10 p.m., twenty dollars starting at eleven. Five-dollar reentry fee. *This business does not con-done human trafficking. Ladies come first, no sex, no touching, no camera phone use, no drugs, no weapons, you must tip if standing around the stage. No chairs around the stage.*

Naughty Nights Lingerie. Katie's Studios. Photography Graphics. Phillip's Furniture. Beauty Land Supply. Cream-colored bricks fallen to the sidewalk.

He drives from Wilson Avenue to Eight Mile and passes an old cemetery on the border of Prichard and Mobile. Cleaned up. Had been weeds over the graves. Looked bad. It's one of the cheapest graveyards around. Many folks from the Village have been buried here. No one section. Wherever they have a space. White plastic sticks serve as temporary grave markers until the families of the deceased can afford a headstone. Da'Cino doesn't like funerals. If he knows someone who died, he just wants to be left alone. He wonders if other people feel the same way. Just cremate me, Da'Cino thinks. I don't want to be in the ground. Pour me out on a basketball court and don't confuse me with flour and bake a cake. He laughs. Has that ever happened? He bet it has.

Da'Cino drives back to Wilson Avenue, calls his brother Marco.

Where you at? Marco asks.

Riding around.

I'm at the barber shop, bro.

Get your hair shaved off, Da'Cino says.

No, man. Get off the phone, man, you crazy. Whatcha doing?

Just driving. Storm coming. Windy out here.

It was blowing last nights.

It got cold last night, man.

Da'Cino notices Big White Wings Restaurant, Maurice

White, proprietor. Inflation was killing him. Seen a big drop off in customers. Didn't know if he'd stay in business, didn't know from one day to the next if he was going to order fries. Deliveries all off. Gets what he can to keep his doors open.

Da'Cino continues on past the square buildings of a tax service company and Hoffman Furniture Company, *permanently closed*; past Exclusive Hair Design, open Tuesday, Wednesday, and Saturday, 10:30 a.m. to 6 p.m. Thursday and Friday, 8:30 a.m. to 6 p.m.; past The Tree Bar-B-Que and Lounge on Lovejoy Loop and Wholesale Shoe Warehouse, *permanently closed*; past Carrie's Tax Service, *temporarily closed* and The Spot, *temporarily closed*; past the broken glass of another vacant store, and a sign announcing, *Coffee Shop coming soon*, and beside it, Flava's Bar and Lounge, and a banner: So many places to go, prison ain't one.

Looking out the window, Da'Cino sees a memory in every bush, every street and house and storefront. That road there, the one curving out of sight with the trees on either side of it, he knows it, was on it with Marco and their stepdad Joe one night years ago. They were driving up a hill about forty miles an hour, low on gas, and Joe had this crazy idea: He told Marco and Da'Cino to jump out and push the van while it still had momentum to get it over the hilltop before it ran out of gas. The boys did anything Joe told them. He didn't slow down or nothing. They jumped out, fat little boys rolling on the pavement scraped from their noses to their feet, running to catch a fifteen-passenger van. By the time they reached it, the van had stopped.

Remember the time, Marco, when Joe made us jump out of the van?

Hell, yeah. He was like: Y'all better not let this van stop.

I'm going to call Joe, make you push that van again, Da'Cino says.

Shoot. Get off the phone, man.

And then we had a car without a floor on the passenger side, remember?

Yeah, an LTD.

At the red lights, we'd stick our feet out.

Like the Flintstones! Marco says.

Man, we did some dumb junk.

Da'Cino laughs. He passes Crawdads, a restaurant. Order today, get your food tomorrow. They're that slow. Fry Daddy's and Fat Boys restaurants nearby. They're not bad. Da'Cino turns onto Highway 45 again. He sees another car wash and next to it the convenience store where he first saw a man shot to death. Nearby, My Boy's Food Market Liquor. Joe made him panhandle outside of it. No one will give a grown man money, but they will give to a kid. Da'Cino hated it. He felt so embarrassed.

Hey Marco, remember when Jamichael threw that can and hit you in the head.

Don't talk to me about that mess, bro.

He should have gone pro with that arm.

Get off my phone, man.

Marco makes Da'Cino laugh, and he's smart too. Da'Cino doesn't understand why he won't apply himself. He holds a job for three months, has his little bit of money, and then he's like, I'm done. He has worked more jobs than Da'Cino but he keeps quitting. Their older brother, Jamichael, is a gofer at a casino. If people need fresh towels, new sheets he runs and gets them. He sticks with jobs. Somewhat. He got fired from one because someone accused him of harassment. The guy was talking smack about Jamichael and after Jamichael confronted him, the guy went to HR, and they fired him. Jamichael has two kids; Marco has three, two in Mississippi and one in Tennessee. Neither of them cares for their children, for real. Following in the footsteps of their daddy. Da'Cino doesn't want to walk in or near those footsteps, but his brothers are doing just that. Marco would steal your name if he could. If a pair of Da'Cino's shoes fit him, Marco will take them. Da'Cino bought them but they both will wear them. He'd snatch Da'Cino's underwear if he could. He got like that from Joe.

Remember when we used to throw food out for the dog?

Max, Marco says.

Yeah, and I slipped on some grits we gave him on my bike. Skid my whole foot up trying to stop. Grits was in the road and the back wheels wouldn't stop so I just slid.

You needed training.

Shut up, I knew how to ride.

Almost a country song, slipped on some grits.

Da'Cino laughs. He and Marco came up together, endured all that mess. They have a bond but Da'Cino still doesn't trust him.

6

As Da'Cino cruises Prichard, sixty-five-year-old Deborah Lacey sits inside her apartment across from a tapestry on the kitchen wall of her son Mayo. The blue light of her big-screen TV illuminates her living room. She left Alabama Village with her grandchildren after Mayo died. She hopes Jamez lives a better life. She tells him right from wrong. His older brother, Jeremiah, moved to Atlanta with his daddy. He'll turn eighteen soon and graduate from high school. He calls her every day. His younger brother, Jerry, got caught with marijuana and a judge referred him to a drug program for six months. Miz Deborah took the boys in just after they were born. Their momma, her daughter, was off into other things. Not drugs, just running wild. Still is.

Miz Deborah always thinks of Mayo. He'd just come from his girlfriend's place and had pulled up to his house when someone shot him from a pickup with a 9 mm pistol. You killed him! she screamed. Miz Deborah spent days afterward walking and weeping. She lost her mind for a minute and has still not recovered. A niece took her in. Mayo sold a little bit of weed but everybody did. Miz Deborah doesn't understand anything anymore.

A small, eight-month-old dog the size of a Chihuahua with long, brown hair scrambles in circles on her lap. Miz Deborah named her Kizzy. The dog reminds her of Mayo. Hyped up just like him. When he was a boy, he participated in the ministry's after-school programs and summer camp, and he attended church on Sundays. In those days, Miz Deborah worked at a Wendy's and cleaned offices. Then she got shot and had to quit. It was a big help to have Mayo at Light of the Village because she couldn't handle him all day while she recovered. It wasn't no bad wound but bad enough, she supposes. Two people started shooting at each other just as she stepped off a bus. She hadn't walked but a minute when a bullet entered the calves of both her legs. It didn't hurt, but it burned something awful. The bus driver called 911. Miz Deborah was laid up for a good little while.

Alabama Village has been rough for so long it's hard for her to say when it started going downhill. People move in to a vacant house, have the power turned on but don't pay rent. Nobody inspects houses in the Village. They've been abandoned, so poor people move in. Miz Deborah doesn't know who lives in Mayo's house now.

She has seen just two shootings—Mayo's and her own—and that was enough. It scares her. She stays out of the way. She was caught in that cross fire once and that was once too many.

Miz Deborah can't hardly remember her younger days. She grew up in Prichard but not in the Village, and was into a little bit of everything. Whatever wasn't tied down she stole, money mostly. Never broke into houses. She robbed people on the street. No guns. She was afraid of guns. Instead she used a bat or a stick, whatever was available to intimidate people. She spent five years in the Julia Tutwiler Prison for

Women and learned to leave stuff alone that didn't belong to her and to live a better life if she didn't want to spend it in jail. She kept her head down and got into a work release program making baskets in a Birmingham factory. Then the prison placed her with a telemarketing company that sold light bulbs but that didn't work out so good. Customers would often cuss, become irrational and worse. Company rules forbade her to respond in kind but she did, more than once, and she went back to making baskets. She never could tolerate anyone lacking manners.

Miz Deborah tells her grandchildren how crazy she was at their age and where it led. She told Mayo the same thing. Sometimes he listened; sometimes he didn't.

7

Slouched behind the wheel, Bigg Man drives his red Dodge Charger past Light of the Village to his house on the south end of Baldwin Drive. He rents an apartment next door to Paul and Lisa McGuire, a white couple. Paul tries to get him to cut his grass because of all the work he did for him when he could walk. They've been in the Village since Bigg Man can remember. He often sees Lisa walking to the Family Dollar on Wilson to buy cigarettes. She says hello in a thick drawl, her mouth a tangle of broken teeth, and hits him up for cigarettes. She calls him Corey. He doesn't object.

Paul spends his days in a wheelchair or in bed in the front room. He wears a brace on his right leg, a vestige of polio, and he has trouble breathing from years of smoking. Liver problems too, from drinking. Beer mostly. Budweiser.

A jumble of thoughts and memories clutter Paul's mind this evening. Can't help but think when all he does is sit. He misses the food stand in Saraland, about a fifteen-minute drive from Prichard, the one in front of Walmart. It had fresh peaches every day, real soft, and nice grapes, good grapes. When he used to drive to the grocery store, that fruit stand was his last stop. Got potatoes, raisins, wheat bread, and cinnamon bread, a dollar each for the loaves. Tomatoes about so big around, and strawberries, too.

His neighbor Ben fished a lot and enjoyed riding a bicycle. There was a guy named "Blind John." He had one eye and drank too much. He had a wife and kids and used to visit Paul. His friend Phil, all he does is call. He never drops by. Paul tries to get him to cut his grass because of all that work he did for him when he could walk, trimming his yard and fixing his lawn mowers and all, but Paul never sees him.

They used to cut fifteen, maybe twenty yards together. Phil would come by the house and Paul would get his Weedwacker and put it in Phil's pickup. Lisa would stay home. Paul used heavy, thick line for his weedwacker; it cut anything. When Phil's stuff got tore up, Paul would walk to his house and work on it. He learned how to fix things by repairing lawn mowers.

He sure would like to walk again. His doctor told him, Well, I ain't never seen nobody who ain't walked in two years get up and walk. Paul said, Well you don't know me doc, and you don't know my boss above. He knows more about me than you do.

What? Lisa asks.

Nothing. I'm just thinking out loud, Paul says.

Bigg Man brings the McGuires food, enough for one meal. Not every day but often. Tonight, he parks in front of their old wood house paled gray by decades of sun. He observes how it lists to one side as if an invisible force is pressing against it. A yellow tarp covers one section and brown leaves float in buckets of rainwater. He gets out of his car with two plastic shopping bags and walks up cracked, concrete steps to the sagging porch. A red rug hangs off the warped railing and a rusted air-conditioning unit takes up a window. Plywood boards and aluminum siding cover other windows.

Bigg Man knocks on the door and waits for the resulting commotion of hysterical barking to subside. Inside, Lisa screams, Shut up! Shut up!, at her two mongrel dogs, Whitey and Lucy and herds them out into an overgrown backyard waist-high with weeds, a cigarette with a long string of ash bobbing from a corner of her mouth. Shutting the door she doubles over from a hacking cough. The ash floats to her feet.

She raises her head and takes a deep breath. Her blue blouse hangs off her emaciated chest, the nubs of her shoulders pressing against the fabric. A freezer in the bedroom is stuffed with smokes. Doctors have diagnosed her with COPD. Started smoking when her daughter died at home in 2014, just fourteen years old. She had cerebral palsy. Was in a wheelchair her whole life, unable to walk or speak. Stayed in the house when she was not in school because Lisa worried she'd get sick, exposed to germs and all. She was a good student. Lisa never took to sitting in a classroom. Not really. She just didn't. She hated math, that was one thing. Completed the tenth grade and told herself: No more.

Lisa unlocks the front door and Bigg Man steps in and fills the room. She says nothing to him. The rotted wood floors hold odors from dog piss, a sharp ammonia reek but he makes no comment. Paul and Lisas see cars lined up outside his house at all times of the day and night, and they assume he's into something illegal, but they don't ask questions.

Lisa saw you coming and told me, Paul says to Bigg Man. That's why I told her you could come in. I always said if just anybody comes to the door don't unlock it, keep the door locked 'cause you got dogs here to protect you. Don't ever let nobody in that door if you don't know them. If you know them that's fine.

It's my family, my brothers and stuff, that's all I let in, and you, Lisa says raising her chin toward Bigg Man.

I knew a black guy stayed across the street, Wayne, he would come over here, Paul says. We'd get food stamps and he'd come over and want cheese and drinks and stuff like that. Told us he'd pay us back. Never did.

He told me to wash his clothes, Lisa says in an indignant voice. A big pile. I ain't washing them no more. Another guy, Ken, he owes me money too for washing his clothes. And another guy lived down there names Huck he owes me money for washing his clothes.

I mostly stay on the phone, watch a little TV, Paul says. If I was in good shape, I'd be out in the yard cleaning up things.

I spend the day cutting up bills and wash clothes, Lisa says. I don't like people to get my name.

I had gastric bypass surgery. They trying to say I had cirrhosis of the liver but the doctors don't know yet. I'll leave it in the good Lord's hands. I'm hoping everything will be all right.

You started feeling bad the year COVID came, Lisa says.

My health turned before that, about ten years before.

Bigg Man shifts silently from one foot to the other, the floors creaking beneath him. Broken ceiling tile above his head. Cobwebs thread the cracked walls, layer photographs of Paul and Lisa when they were young, their smiles not yet diminished, frozen in a better time. The funeral program for their daughter stands open on a shelf. A photo shows her black hair, pouting lips. *Jennifer Marie McGuire, aged 15, native to Mobile, Alabama, resident of Chickasaw, Alabama, departed this life on Sunday, November 3, 2014, at her home. Jennifer is survived by her parents Paul and Lisa McGuire.* Lisa and Paul were sitting with her when she died. Blood ran from her mouth. Lisa called her momma. Get the paramedics, her momma said. By the time the ambulance arrived, Jennifer had passed. Morning. Gone. She had crawled into bed smiling twelve hours earlier. Gave Lisa a kiss good night and all. Lisa doesn't think a mother recovers from something like that. Paul cries at the memory.

Paul is sixty-seven; Lisa is forty-seven. They grew up in the Village. Paul's daddy joined the navy before Paul was born. He was there for Pearl Harbor and served in World War II. He worked on tugboats after his discharge. As a boy, Paul lived on Fayette Street. The house is still there. Go on Baldwin to Dunlap, a right at a gas station, take that first street to the left and the house will be sitting there. Back then he knew of only one Black person in the Village, Mr. Will, an older fellow. He was a good washing machine man. Dryers and everything else. He died a couple years ago.

Paul met Lisa at a high school football game at Prichard Stadium, now closed. Lisa's brother Mike, a friend of Paul's, introduced them and they just started talking. He asked her if she wanted to go with him to the park and she said, Yeah. Afterward he took her to his house in Chickasaw. She had a job at the dog track, Mobile Greyhound Park, and couldn't stay long because she worked five at night to five in the morning. Paul started taking her to work. He thought she was real pretty when she got all dressed up.

Paul coached football for years at Hamilton Middle School. Youth football too. Lisa would help keep score. Paul still hears from a few of his old players. Some of them did well. Roosevelt Patterson played for the University of Alabama. The New England Patriots selected Kevin Lee in the second round of the 1994 NFL draft. Amari Cooper played with the Dallas Cowboys.

Paul never played football because of his polio, however, he loved kids. He was a strict coach but fair. You can't pop a kid on the head because he did something wrong, you got to sit him down and talk to him, Paul would tell other coaches. Teach him to do it the right way, not the wrong way. Teach him how to run, teach him how to block, teach him how to hold the ball, teach him that if you win a game, you win; if you lose, you lose. He reminded his players: You're out here to have fun.

He and Lisa bought their house in 1996 for $8,000. At the time, Paul fixed watches and repaired outdoor power tools. A duplex once stood in the lot across the street but after it sold, someone burned it down. Next door, a Black guy bought that house and the gray one too, where Bigg Man lives, and the same man purchased another house a little ways further down on Baldwin about where it turns toward the Light of the Village.

Paul knows his house needs repairs but he hasn't been able to do the work because of his health. He hopes to get a ramp built. He fell out of his wheelchair on his front porch one day, hit the guardrail and hurt his neck. Lisa called the paramedics. Took them two, three hours to arrive. Well, maybe not that long but long.

I'd miss the memories but other than that I wouldn't miss nothing else, Paul says. We been talking about getting out of here but I can't afford six hundred to eight hundred dollars a month to rent a house. That will take about my whole check. We're both on disability but that's not enough to pay the water bill or power bill. It's been her family and my family telling us to get a better place. Well, if you find us a better place we'll go, I told them. You going to pay for it?

Look at our water bill, Lisa says. I paid $138 but the check bounced. Now its $238. We need some help to pay that. We don't have the money to pay that no way. That's for two months. We ain't got the money in the bank. It's ridiculous.

Everything we own belongs to God, Paul says.

Then he can pay the water bill, Lisa says.

People building this and that and charging crazy rents. As far as Paul's concerned they'd better get serious. They don't know when God's going to come down. In the twinkling of an eye the clouds could bust wide open. What's all them people charging those crazy rents going do when God sticks his hand through a cloud and says, It's time? They'll go crazy. Do you know what you're looking at buddy? That's Jesus Christ. If you ready, there he is. People don't realize. Money isn't going to get them to heaven. They can't take it with them when they go.

Are you a churchgoing man? Paul asks Bigg Man.

I believe in God, Bigg Man says.

One day, Paul tells him, when Lisa was sick with the flu, he went to Destination Church in Saraland to pray for her. He could still drive at the time. Maybe five, six years ago. He sat in a back pew. Two ladies—they might've been twins, they looked so alike—walked past him. One of them dropped a one-hundred-dollar bill in the offering plate. Paul gave a little old, rumpled dollar bill. The woman took his hand, held it over the plate and he felt a piece of paper rise into his palm. He closed his fist but didn't look at it. The woman released his hand, and just like that she and the other lady disappeared. Paul glanced around but couldn't find them. He shoved the paper into his pocket. After the service, he walked to his car, reached into his pocket and withdrew a crumpled one-hundred-dollar bill. No lie, he told Bigg Man. When he returned home, he took Lisa to Walmart for flu medication. A man standing in line at the register tapped her on the shoulder. Do you mind if I give you this? No, it's up to you, Lisa said. What is it? He placed a one-hundred-dollar bill in her hand. Lisa looked up to thank him but he had vanished. That man and the ladies at the church had to be angels, Paul told Bigg Man. Had to be. We were in need and God sent them to us.

Bigg Man doesn't comment. He hefts the bags filled with chicken, lima beans, and rice and walks across the living room to the kitchen and places them on the counterwhich has separated from the wall. He stares down at the black ground beneath it. The dogs bark. Bigg Man retraces his steps through the living room to the front door.

Thank you, man, Paul says.

Bigg Man doesn't answer. Paul and Lisa watch him. He steps onto the porch and pullsthe door shut behind him.

—⁓—

Bigg Man crosses the McGuire's yard to his house. Asleep, he dreams of homeboys dying, and then they die for real. Like a guy everyone called "Dirty." Bigg Man dreamed about him getting shot, and two months later someone killed him. He has dreams of getting shot himself. The bad stuff in his dreams comes true. He wishes he could leave the Village. He wishes he didn't need to sleep. He wishes he could stop dreaming.

8

As the night deepens, a pale light illuminates the Lighthouse porch and greets Da'Cino when he returns. On one of several nearby trees, a cracked two-by-four scrawled with the message, *Holy Spirit I have You*, hangs unevenly. Arthur James Williams Sr., better known as Mr. Arthur, nailed up that sign and dozens more like it—*Holy Spirit I have you; Let It Shine, Lord; Wow*—all around the Village.

In 2018, the host of the radio program *Our Southern Souls* interviewed Mr. Arthur. A photo on the program's website showed him to be a middle-aged Black man missing most of his teeth. He had a wide smile and his eyes shined with delight. He had lost most of his hair.

Mr. Arthur said he started making the signs after his house burned down a few years before the interview. A friend pulled him out but he sustained injuries. He believed God had spared him and he began making the signs to express his gratitude.

You walk by the signs and something comes over you. It changes people. They have told me it does. Some people tell me to stop. I can't stop making these signs. I am hooked on God, he told the host of *Our Southern Souls*.

He put signs up every day. A feeling would just come over him compelling him to do it. He had worked as a maintenance man and an animal control officer in Prichard. He had been married but his wife had died. He had many children. He liked to drink but prayed for God to lead him toward sobriety. He died of alcoholism in 2020.

More declarations of Mr. Arthur's faith—*I walk and sing, Walk with me Lord, Walk with me. Take my hand Lord and walk with me*—fill trees leading to Restoration Youth Academy and the classroom Mr. Tommie has turned into his home. Blue pools of moonlight illuminate shards of broken glass and corroded shell casings in what had been the academy's parking lot.

A concrete walk leads through chest-high shrubs to a one-story building. Mr. Tommie stands at the entrance. Stroking his graying goatee, he runs his other hand through his thick hair. Two black, long underwear shirts and a worn black sweatshirt cover his narrow chest and match his black jeans. The holes in his sneakers reveal his toes. A warm night, he thinks. He doesn't believe it will stay hot. Got some bad weather coming, rain, thunderstorm maybe. He feels it in the air.

He doesn't worry about rain because his ceiling doesn't suffer from leaks. The corner where he keeps his firewood gets a few drops but nothing more. He doesn't know what he'll cook tonight. He has consumed so many canned goods, there should be nary a canned good left on the planet. For the last seven years. That's a lot of canned goods.

On a railing, he adjusts the assortment of pots he uses for collecting rainwater to wash his clothes and dishes. The other day he cleared a bare patch of ground to plant onions and watermelon. He'll have to wait until June. Too early yet. Might get another frost. Not likely but possible. Frost will kill onions and watermelon.

He needs to collect wood before the rain starts. He has a small pile, but will burn through it in a minute. Winter ain't done with him yet. He has lived in the academy for four years. Four or five. When it gets cold, it gets real cold. The cold clings to these bare walls. Warmer outside than it is in.

Strangers come around but not lately. He has grown so used to being alone it shocks him when they do. The last person to surprise him came through four months ago. Tommie caught him looking around in one of the buildings but he left without explanation. A stripped car has been in the parking lot for months. Tommie always thinks next time he sees a Prichard cop, he'll flag him down and tell him about it but he never sees them, not around here. They stay on Highway 45 and Eight Mile, the better parts of town.

He knows a man who has lived under a bridge for six years. Got a nice little setup. Safe. Don't get wet in the rain but just the idea of living like that and dealing with all the cars and trucks rattling over his head would bother Tommie. He'll stick with what he has.

Tommie was born in Choctaw County way up Highway 45, a good three hours from Prichard. His momma moved with him and his four sisters to Prichard in the 1970s. Their father stayed behind. Tommie was about twelve then, no, more like eight or nine. They lived in a two-bedroom Section 8 house. The man who owned the place, a white dude, sold drugs and went to prison, and someone else took over the property.

In those days, Black people didn't go to the Village. Couldn't even walk up Baldwin. White people would jump them. Tommie was bused to school from Prichard to Chickasaw. White kids threw rocks and there were fights every day. Tommie got in a couple. The teachers were nice, just the white students were tripping. He completed the eleventh grade before he dropped out. He was never into book learning.

As the decades passed, the violence increased in Prichard. Tommie's momma got tired of all the shooting. Too many bullets hit the house, including one that went through Tommie's bedroom. He and his momma moved to Mobile in 2000 and lived in a little green one-story house. His sisters had married but not Tommie. Not even close. His momma watched him. As a boy, she wouldn't let him play with other kids to keep him out of trouble. When the sun went down he had to be inside. By the time he was grown, he had become used to living a secluded life and saw no reason to change. Went out with friends every now and then but not often. He has no children. Good thing. So many have kids, and their parents can't care for them. That's one worry he won't have to shoulder.

Tommie cooked three times a day for his momma. Rice, collard greens, baked chicken, cornbread, Tommie made it all. They had a stove, refrigerator, bathtub, the whole works. That was good living. His momma couldn't eat fried food. She loved the baked chicken sold at a diner on Hosfelt Lane.

He still cooks; loves black-eyed peas. Greens are good but shrink. He continues to bake cornbread. Put some meal, flour, and water in a plastic bowl, stir it up real good. Put it on the grill. Ten minutes, it's done. He gets his water from Light of the Village.

While his momma was alive, Tommie worked as a garbageman for the city of Chickasaw, a job he enjoyed. Constantly moving, never bored. Nice coworkers, nice customers. People gave him food and money on holidays. Mr. Hall of Hall's Sausage and Wholesale Meats used to hand out hot sausages all the time. Tommie picked through trash he collected for copper and aluminum, bundled it, and put it on the side of the road to pick up after work and sell it to recycling centers. Aluminum paid about five cents a pound; copper paid two dollars to five dollars a pound. Tommie's challenge was to sort the aluminum, separating the clean material from the «dirty» pieces containing attached steel. Clean aluminum brought a better price. There used to be a scrap place near the Village but the state shut it down. The owner had the scales rigged and cheated people out of their money. Tommie thinks a lot of them still do that, but they know not to be so obvious about it.

One evening, he returned home from work and his older sister asked, Where have you been? I found momma on the floor. She's been like that all day. Tommie quit his job and took care of her. When she died, it was like someone snatched the rug out from under him. He stayed at the house and worked for the landlord in exchange for rent but the Section 8 housing voucher had been in his mother's name and eventually the landlord told him to leave. He painted the house, cleaned it out, and the landlord returned the deposit.

He moved to the Bama Motel on Government Boulevard; $228 a month. It had a bathroom, kitchenette, and a big bed that took up most the room. His former landlord would pick him up in the morning three times a week to do odd jobs. After eleven months, he had no more work. He gave Tommie a little extra money and a bicycle. Tommie submitted job applications but no one hired him and he didn't have transportation anyway. A bicycle would only take him so far. Tommie could no longer afford his room. At that point he considered himself homeless. He remembers the date, April 1, 2014.

A white guy he knew from Daphne told him he needed someone to watch his eighty-year-old mother. Why don't you stay with her? he suggested, and Tommie agreed. She lived in a trailer and he moved in to an RV nearby. She told him to call her Miz Burke. She had rare plants, the names of which Tommie no longer recalls. At least she said they were rare, and she owned thirty little dogs, Chihuahua-like things. She wasn't the cleanest lady. They crapped all over. She'd buy a big old bag of tobacco and roll cigarettes in this little machine she had. In the evenings, she'd call Tommie and they would drink a little wine and she'd smoke a cigarette surrounded by dogs and plants and talk him to death. Her son-in-law didn't like the idea of a stranger staying with her and he told Tommie to leave. It only takes one person to ruin a good deal. He got on his bike and survived by being an itinerant handyman.

Tommie discovered the academy by chance. One night in 2018 he stopped in a field to sleep. About two in the morning it started raining. Crawling out of his sleeping bag, Tommie got on his bicycle and started riding in no particular direction seeking shelter. He saw the square-shaped buildings of the academy through the rain shined by moonlight. He rode toward them and has been here ever since. Took him a minute to clean out the room he now calls home. He moved mountains of debris, mostly broken ceiling tiles, and piled it in a hall where it remains, a testimony to his labor. Then he swept and swept, dust swirling around him in ankle-high windstorms, until a blue carpet emerged. He hung plastic sheets where there had once been walls. One window provides light and overlooks his vegetable garden. He used to see rabbits and possums but hasn't seen either one in months except as roadkill on Wilson Avenue. People swerve and hit them on purpose. Some folks are just born mean.

Coons eat all the trash and scare away everything else that hasn't been hit by a car including dogs. Dogs won't mess with a coon. The smart ones anyway. Won't be long before someone comes and hauls the burned bus for scrap. Or maybe it will continue sitting there like the car until it becomes part of the woods.

He has a sleeping bag and a mosquito net inside an oblong tent. Like crawling into a coffin. The hard floor kills his back. He found a mattress and that helps a little. He likes to lay down and listen to his radio. As long as he has batteries, it will provide him with company. He'd be talking to himself without it. He gets lonely, he ain't lying. The radio helps but sometimes he can't put up with it and shuts it off and the silence comforts him until it doesn't.

A firepit lined with aluminum siding takes up one corner where he also keeps mousetraps. He catches rats, big ones, and hears them in the walls. One of them walked into a trap about three in the morning. Tommie didn't get up. Hours later, he kicked out of his sleeping bag and checked the trap but it was gone. Must've been a huge rat to run off with a trap. He sees a lot of crows when he wakes up but as the day goes on they leave before the shooting starts. Didn't fly all this way to get blasted out of the sky. He laughs at his own humor.

Fishing calendars given to him by the manager of a Chickasaw hardware store cover the one wall adjacent to his sleeping bag. The calendars provide the companionship of good memories. Tommie loves to fish. He caught a barracuda in the Gulf one time, not a great eating fish and the big ones have a lot of mercury. Same with tuna. The bigger the fish, the more mercury they carry. He has caught redfish, a good eating fish. Croaker too, a better eating fish. He likes sheepshead almost as much. He snagged one the size of a plate years ago, a big son of a gun.

He likes to bicycle to Chickasabogue Creek in Chickasaw in
the morning and fish. Can get a little chilly on the water. Get
around a lot of trees; that helps block the wind. Stays real quiet.
No kind of mess. Seagulls float on the currents. All the birds
come out early. Other fishermen have told Tommie they've
seen manatees in the creek. That would be something. Used
to have otters, jet-black ones. He hasn't seen them for a while.

Tommie has caught all kinds of fish on the creek. Perch,
channel cat, bluegill, spotted bass, white crappie. Walleye. What
else? Yellow perch. Bream. Redfish. Flathead, whitehead, striped
bass. Puts lizards on his hooks; they make good fish bait. Sit
on a bench, watch turtles sunning side by side on moss-draped
branches, listen to the breeze, the rustling leaves. A guy used to
rent boats. He moved on but he made a good little bit of money.
Elderly people walk their dogs near the water's edge. He saw a
man put a little suit on his dachshund. Tommie fell out laughing.

Last year he met some dudes from Vietnam. He told them
his situation and they gave him food and he sat down and ate
with them. One of them gave him thirty dollars.

A meth head named David lived in one of the buildings
behind Tommie. He's been gone now for a minute and Tommie
doesn't miss him. He believed in Satan. He had written on the
walls *I love Satan*. All night long he was in and out, in and out.
Weird, man. Satan didn't teach him to clean. He lived worse than
a pig. It was a good day when David left and the devil with him.

Tommie uses an office outside his door as a prayer room. A
crucifix and a picture of Jesus hang on the wall. Lying in his tent
one night, Tommie heard the Holy Spirit tell him, Build you a
room to pray, and he did. Every morning, before he does anything
else, he reads the Bible, and then rides his bike to collect cans. He
sells them for about thirty-seven cents a pound. In the evening,

he smokes his room to kill bugs. He sits in the warmth of the airy heat looking out at the gathering dusk before he douses the fire. He doesn't want the light to attract the wrong people.

He misses renting a house. He'd watch CNN all day long if he did. He saw President Donald Trump on TV one afternoon in 2007 when he went to a friend's house to borrow their phone. He never saw Joe Biden except once on TV when he was vice president. Tommie can't picture his face. He assumes he's changed a lot since then. He's never seen a photo of his former vice president Kamala Harris.

He enjoyed talking to one of his sisters in St. Louis about what he saw on CNN. She was a newshound like him. She died in her sleep four days after Christmas 2020. Tommie didn't find out for two months. A white lady in Chickasaw he'd known for some years told him. You need to call Dale, she said, referring to his brother-in-law. Why, what's up? Just get ahold of Dale, she said. He did and Dale left word for him. His sister had been buried and everything by then. Dale said he hadn't known how to reach him but Tommie didn't believe him. Dale just didn't try. Sylvia Jones Robinson. Just died in her sleep. Natural death. And here he is homeless and still alive.

Last night, he had an idea: If he could scrape enough money together, two or three thousand dollars, he'd buy a small lot and then get a trailer or a camper. Plenty of them around and reasonably priced too. That would solve his housing problem. Might not even have to buy a lot. He could rent one. Miz Julia has a front yard. He'd set it there if she'd let him. Maybe pay her two hundred a month. He wouldn't want to be in her house but outside in a trailer. He'll think about it. Have to come up with the money first. Miz Julia isn't dealing with a full deck but he likes her. That guy staying with her takes advantage. Men like that say they're waiting on their money and when they get their check she never sees them again. He'll have a word with her. A camper should be doable pricewise. Make payments once a month, he could do that. He'd want a nice one if he could hustle the cash. A person got to have money. They can't just pick up and leave with nothing. Where will they go? Takes money to move and get set up elsewhere or they'll end up in the same situation they were in but worse.

He found a space heater the other day. Clean, real nice. Reconnected two wires to get it working again. Plugged it in at the church and it started right up. He was sure Cash America Pawn in Saraland would give him twenty bucks for it, but the owner only gave him ten.

Springtime, he explained to Tommie. The days'll be getting warmer.

Tommie looked down at the counter and made a face. He heard Tom Petty singing "Running Down a Dream" from a speaker in the ceiling and wondered when he had last heard that song. Tom Petty's been dead a minute. Tommie found a magazine by the church dumpster that mentioned he'd passed.

I'm already selling air conditioners, the owner said.

That's a good heater for whoever gets it, Tommie said.

I'll sell it for twenty. You get ten, I get ten.

If I had my own place I'd keep the heater, Tommie said. I'd use it for the bathroom. Wouldn't let it fall in my tub when I'm in the shower.

The owner laughed.

Actually, that's a myth, he said. Generally, if it fell in your tub it would blow a fuse. You'd probably get shocked and if you had a heart issue you might die from that. It generally won't electrocute you to death.

I'm not going to test your theory, Tommie said.

You ain't joking, the owner said.

Tommie accepted his offer. Ten dollars was better than no dollars. Not bad for something he found on a trash pile. Cost him a little time to fix that was all. Without pawnshops, people would be in real trouble. Gas is up, food is up, and none of it is coming back down. It's good to spend money but you want something for it. Twenty dollars for a steak. Crazy. He loves chicken wings but they've gone way up. When he receives his food stamps next month, he might splurge and buy some.

The noise of gunfire no longer bothers him unless bullets strike close to his room. A bullet pierced six stucco pillars six feet apart outside his door one time. *Bam, bam, bam.* Tommie dropped and rolled against a wall. Then the shooting stopped. A lot of people tote guns. He wonders how they afford them. Bullets ain't cheap. Big guns too, .357s, .44s, and others, like machine guns. He found some candles but he won't use them, not at night when the wrong people might see them burning and think he has money. What would happen when they realized he didn't? He'd rather not know. He listens in the dark for noises he doesn't recognize.

Tommie takes his bicycle from the wall and pushes it outside. No place to go, he just wants to get out. Maybe collect a few cans. He walks along the academy driveway to Escambia Street. He feels wrung out. Every day and every night he asks God to get him out of this place. Find me some clothes, shoes, socks, and a roof over my head. Get me a real good hot tub of water. He looks around, recognizes pine trees but doesn't know the names of the other trees but he's sure they're called something. He'll have to learn what they are. He saw a buzzard and a hawk one morning above the trees. Beautiful. So high in the sky. He watched them soar with envy.

He considers one of Mr. Arthur's signs, *God Is Intense.* So many signs. They're everywhere. Kind of creepy. Tommie believes he may have met Mr. Arthur. A Black guy big on Jesus stopped him one day and gave him fifty dollars. Just up and gave it to him and kept going on about Jesus.

I'm blessed, thank the Lord, I'm blessed, he said.

Pray for me, Tommie asked him.

I will, brother, the man said. Pray for me too.

Tommie never saw him again. He stretched that fifty like a rubber band.

9

Dolores worries about Mr. Tommie. She wonders what he does for food, how he keeps warm in winter. He doesn't seem to want help. She enjoys talking to him. He's very sweet and polite and appears at peace. One time he had trouble with his bike and she and John replaced a tire. When he stops and checks in, she gives him food. Mostly she tries to be kind and offer him company.

She misses Mr. Arthur. She remembers him as a gentle soul who professed a deep faith. He loved God but he drank until he was intoxicated, and then he beat himself up for displeasing God. He had a huge heart but he was torn. He told Dolores he wanted to do better but his alcoholism held him back. He was a tall man, about six one, but not heavy. What hair he had he tied into a braid. His expressive eyes danced with joy or drooped with sorrow depending upon his mood and the amount of alcohol he had consumed. He could fix things and helped out at the church. He dropped by and swept and mopped according to his whims. He would arrive in a good mood or walk in weeping. Dolores would take him in a room and give him Kleenex and they would talk and pray.

Mr. Arthur spread the Gospel using his signs. It's all but impossible to drive through the Village and not see one. Dolores wrote down what he wanted to say on a piece of paper and he'd copy it onto a board with markers she provided. It amazed her how many he put up. He scavenged discarded boards from the woods. In the fall and winter, the bare branches holding his signs declared his faith. *Oh, Lord, I'm Coming Home.* When he died in 2020, Dolores felt confident he had.

Da'Cino, Dolores believes, has come far. He was always polite. Quiet, but polite. His stepfather, Joe, didn't really like Dolores or John. She remembers when she first saw him with Da'Cino and his brothers. Dolores asked if she could get them water. Joe said, Yes, and then let them play with the other children. He could be nice in a condescending way. Dolores put up with him so Da'Cino and his siblings would come back.

Billy Boy, on the other hand, just seems lost. Dolores and John have known him since he was a child. He always had a mind of his own and wanted to be seen as a hip, cool dude. However, people watch his actions more than they listen to his words. He doesn't command their respect. They see that he doesn't work or take care of his children. He has to change his life before he can be a role model.

That's the part that saddens Dolores. Billy Boy knows what he should be doing. He talks about it but he doesn't follow through. She and John have sent Billy Boy to several jobs programs but he's always walked out. It's tragic, really. Billy Boy is bright and has insight. His observations about people can be spot on.

One afternoon a preacher approached the basketball court behind the ministry. Guys from all over Prichard were playing. The preacher said, Stop. I want to share the word of God with you. Bow your heads. Who here wants to go to heaven? The players looked at John and he nodded, indicating they should do what he asked in the hope he'd leave. The preacher led them in a prayer of repentance. Billy Boy shuffled next to John. What do you think? John asked him. Is he leading them to Christ?

He's not leading them very far, Billy Boy said.

Dolores hopes Bigg Man drops by again. Was he going to call them about going out, or were she and John supposed to call him? She can't remember. Bigg Man was always a good kid but the streets exerted their pull. He wanted money for shoes and outfits. That never changed even after he buried that one pair of sneakers. Every holiday he'd ask, Miz Dolores, can we get me an outfit, get me these shoes? He wanted to leave a store wearing new clothes. The Fourth of July was not about fireworks or cookouts but walking around in a fresh outfit. Bigg Man never outgrew that.

She remembers when he called John about his son, Corey Jr. Revenge did not come up. Perhaps because the child's mother was present when he died and Bigg Man may still have had feelings for her. After he left the hospital he drove to the church and pulled up in his red car, music blasting. Hey, Mr. John, he shouted. He got out and walked up to him. How come they say my little Corey shot himself? How do a baby shoot themselves in the back of the head? He and John talked for about thirty minutes. John mostly listened. He didn't question Bigg Man's doubts about the shooting. He had doubts himself. He suspected the boyfriend may have shot him by accident, similar to his suspicions of what happened to TJ. Bigg Man was angry but not out of control. Unlike many of the other young men John knew, Bigg Man kept a lid on his impulses. John asked him if he wanted to put his son's photo on the Memorial Wall.

Yes, I want to do it.

When do you want to do it?

Wednesday night, Bigg Man said.

He called ahead of time. John and Dolores lit candles. John asked him where he wanted him to put the photo and Bigg Man showed him. He did not speak. He watched John tape the picture. Then he left without a word.

Dolores thinks he still doesn't understand what happened. She doubts he has asked himself how he may have contributed to the situation. Every young man she knows in the Village thinks they love their kids. She doesn't fault them for not trying harder. They never had an example in their own lives. They don't know about birth control, something Dolores chides herself for not emphasizing more. She doesn't believe they have kids so they can be eligible for higher welfare benefits. They may do some things with the wrong motive, but who hasn't? They live lives different from what most people know.

Now, Jesenda dotes on her children. Dolores remembers how she used to be. Jesenda could fight and would. Once that switch turned on, good luck turning it off. Nothing could stop her. Jesenda had a hot temper. She has come a long way. She exudes joy, and Dolores is so proud of her. Jesenda is smart, always has been. People don't mess with her.

Cindy Darrington was another mother who could not have been more devoted to her children. Everyone called her Miz Cindy. She loved to cook. People would fight over her fried chicken. She liked to joke. She showed all her teeth when she laughed. Just about anything she said was funny. She was real good with children. She looked after them and she would let their mommas know if they acted up.

Her friend, Jacqueline Myles, used to tote a red Brahmin

wallet. Miz Cindy didn't like it. You need to put that nasty wallet up somewhere, she told Jacqueline. One day she came to the house holding a pink wallet with silver rhinestones. I bought you a wallet because I'm tired of you carrying that ugly thing, she said.

Cindy, Jacqueline said, I like my wallet.

No, don't let me see you with that ugly wallet no more. That's an ugly thing.

She took in anyone who needed a meal and a place to stay. She'd give a homeless person a few dollars and encouraging words. Firm but loving. Don't give up. Hang in there. Something like that. Miz Cindy would ask Mr. John to help someone if she couldn't. Hey Mr. John, I got so-and-so in my house and they need this and that. No matter their sins, everyone deserves love, she told her children. She wanted her boys to receive an education, but she also allowed kids into her house who sold drugs and had dropped out of school. Her home became the center of all this junk and her children had to navigate all that, the different guys she dated—and not good guys, either. Jesse would say, I don't like them. Dolores never understood why she let just anybody in. She was so nice; too nice. She couldn't say no and do what was best for her but she loved her children and they adored her. No one questions that.

Miz Cindy understood the dangers of the street and kept the boys in the house as much as she could. She told them to think about what they wanted to do when they were older. Avoid the lure of fast money, she warned them. Jesse promised her he'd enroll in college. His mother cautioned him against having kids unless he was married and had a job to support a family. Mr. John and Miz Dolores told him, Don't slip up.

Every morning before school Miz Cindy made her three

boys read a chapter from the Bible. It could be any chapter. The point was to start their day with God's Word and stay focused despite distractions. If she got mad at the boys, she'd just look at them. She had an intimidating stare. She and the boys attended Bible study. She helped them memorize scripture; she checked in on them. She would be the one to text John and say, Hey would you speak with Jesse. Something seems to be going on. That degree of involvement provided a level of stability that from a middle-class point of view might seem shaky but in the Village offered enough cohesion to endure the chaos, withstand the storm.

Miz Cindy treated people in a respectful, deliberate manner. Quiet. Like Bigg Man but in a gentler way. She knew everybody. It was almost as if she felt bad if her boys got something because of her connection with the church but someone else she knew didn't, and she'd make it a point to call John or Dolores to make sure they included that person. Sometimes, maybe thinking she was asking too much, she'd just take them, tucking it under her blouse. Random stuff: toilet paper, snacks. She was a big woman and could just hide it in whatever she wore. Totally impulsive. Always a staple item. John and Dolores never figured it out. They would have given her those things if she had asked. Maybe she was just embarrassed that she lived where she did. She wasn't oblivious to what went on in the Village: It's worse now but it was crazy then too. She was a good person but not a perfect one. In some ways she contributed to the turbulence her boys encountered because of whom she allowed in the house, a lack of judgment that led to an all-too-familiar ending.

A boyfriend shot her on Friday, December 1, 2017. The church held a memorial for her the following week on a cold, rainy night. She always sat in a specific spot for Bible study. John put candles on her chair and her boys sat around it and arranged more. Many people attended. After the service, everyone went out behind the church to release balloons. The rain had slowed but not stopped. People drifted off but Jesse and John stayed outside, the cool moist air sheathing their faces in mist. One blue balloon hovered about ten feet off the ground. Perhaps it doesn't have enough helium, John thought. It followed a path toward Dunlap Circle, one that Miz Cindy often took, and made a right turn as she would. It caught the glow of streetlights. John and Jesse watched it. It's going up the road like my mom, Jesse said. He turned to John.

Do you believe she's in heaven?

John nodded.

I really do, he said.

I do too, Jesse replied.

10

Morgan had been home in Mobile when she received a text from John that Cindy had been shot. She remembers what she was wearing, a red flannel shirt and blue jeans, and that her hair was up. She sank to the floor. I have to pray now, she thought, for Cindy and her children. They've been thrown into a whirlwind.

11

A day never passes that Jesse doesn't think of his mother. He was seventeen when she died. He speaks of her to anyone who asks, keeping her name alive and safe in his heart. Cindy Denise Darrington. They lived next door to the Village. Jesse would walk through a hole in a fence to see his friends there. At five, he got involved with the ministry. His mother told him, There's a program where people will help you with homework and feed you. Young as he was, Jesse was skeptical. It was not that common to see white people in or around the Village, but John and Dolores held a six-week summer camp and it was fun, and it didn't take long for the color of their skin not to matter.

Before he reached his teens, nine people had died in front of his house. Once, he hadn't yet left for school when he saw a man bleeding on the ground. His mother and a neighbor tried to stanch the blood from the bullet. Jesse stayed in the moment. There's a dead man in the yard. I have to finish breakfast. I have to go to school. I have to catch the bus. He learned to smother his shock. The feelings would eat him up otherwise.

So much dying. Even his brothers, they stopped feeling. They slept through shootings.

His mother told Jesse, Jerel, and her youngest boy, Jeremiah, to think about what they wanted to do when they were older. Avoid the lure of fast money, she urged them. Jesse promised her he'd enroll in college. He started thinking ahead to the next day, the next week, the next month. Even now as he talks, he considers what he wants to do this afternoon. He doesn't know why he thinks this way. To stay out of trouble, maybe. He has homeboys and cousins who try to seduce him into the streets.

C'mon, get in the car, Jesse. Let's do this; let's do that.

Nah, man, I'm good.

Jesse's father didn't involve himself with the family, and Jesse has seen him only a few times. He thinks his father's absence forced him to become a man and assume responsibilities sooner than he might otherwise have.

The night his mother died, Jesse lay in bed chilling. He sent a text to John telling him what he and his brothers wanted for Christmas. He heard Jerel warming food in the microwave. Jeremiah slept. No one outside, no loud car mufflers, a quiet night. Then Jesse heard a bang inside the house and his heart jumped. He leaped to his feet and ran toward the front door, and Jerel slammed into him running from the kitchen, knocking Jesse down momentarily. Jerel fled into Jesse's room and collapsed below a window, shouting, Momma just got killed, Momma just got killed! Jesse bolted down the hall and saw her boyfriend pointing a gun in his direction and he dropped to the floor. He thought he'd been shot but, realizing he had only slipped, leaped back up, ran to his room, closed the door, and pushed a dresser in front of it. Jerel cowered in the corner. Then Jesse remembered Jeremiah. He moved the dresser, opened the door, crept out, and peered into Jeremiah's room. He was asleep. Jesse tried to catch his breath, slow the banging of his heart. He walked down the dim hall and stopped. He saw his mother on the floor, eyes open, blood pooling and the boyfriend gone.

Momma's dead, he wrote in a text to John.

John called him.

What do you mean your mom's dead?

She's been shot, Jesse said.

His voice cracked.

Are you guys safe? Are the police there?

No.

We'll be right there, John said.

He hung up and called the police. After he got off the phone, he found Dolores. We have to go, he said. It was weird. Like doctors, he and Dolores were on call. There's a fire, you're a fireman, go put it out. He didn't understand what had happened. He did and he didn't. He didn't know what he thought. Aw, this can't be right. The police had arrived by the time he and Dolores reached the house. The boys stood outside. No big hugs. John and Dolores talked to them. Are you doing OK? No one asked him to pray. Hey, Mr. John, and that was it. It rained. The boyfriend had turned himself in. John and Dolores stayed until the coroner removed the body.

Jesse and his brothers were in school the next Monday. Picked up their lives and got on with it. Jesse called John the following Saturday, the day of the funeral.

I can't make it to my momma's funeral. Is that alright? I got to take my SAT that morning, Mr. John. The funeral's at eight o'clock. Momma wanted me to go to college so I have to take the test.

Hey Jesse, John said, what if they moved the funeral to two o'clock?

Oh, yeah I can go then.

John rescheduled the funeral, and Morgan drove Jesse to the SAT testing site. When he graduated from high school the next year, he enrolled at Alabama Community College just as he had promised her. Now, he wants to transfer to Auburn University and major in engineering but he needs to earn money first. Auburn won't pay for itself.

Jesse and his brothers live with their maternal grandmother. They help her clean the house and cut the yard. At night, they talk to each other to stay strong and keep it together so their feelings don't boil over and explode. That can happen. The murder of a mother can make people lose their minds, mess with their brains in some way. When people get mad, they don't think, they just do. Everyone has the strength to hold on. It's up to them to maintain or lose control. He and his brothers hold on.

Some of Jesse's classmates don't know about the Village but Jesse can't remove it from his mind. He has flashbacks of the night his mother died and tries to subdue them so he doesn't go crazy. His brothers have bad dreams. Anyone who thinks about something really hard, of course they're going to dream about it. Everyone has nightmares.

12

Billy Boy stops at Mr. Arthur's house on Hale Drive and lets himself in through an unlocked back door. He knew him well. The house became one of Billy Boy's go-to places. If his family couldn't find him, they knew to call Mr. Arthur.

Billy Boy remembers how Mr. Arthur could drink. Outside the hit houses, he and those older cats, man, put down their wine. Started early and didn't bother to eat. Billy Boy used to get on Mr. Arthur about that. Whatcha doing, Mr. Arthur? I know you ain't got no wine in your hands. Not at no eight o'clock in the morning. Tell me I'm not seeing things, Mr. Arthur. He made Billy Boy mad, slowly killing himself like that.

Mr. Arthur burned trash in a barrel outside his house and Billy Boy would warm his hands and then walk inside without knocking, just give a shout, Hey, Mr. Arthur! He used to watch him put up his signs. That was all he did. Hammer and nails. Real old school. Signs everywhere, man, like weeds. He put one on a tree in his front yard where a young woman died. *O, yes, Jesus loves Detoria.* Billy Boy knew her. Some guys started shooting and she got caught in the cross fire and dropped as if a hand rose out of the earth and yanked her down. That was a very bad day. Three people were wounded and Detoria died.

Billy Boy feels Mr. Arthur's presence. One of his rooms has a desk and a lectern where he'd preach to whoever dropped by. A taxidermied deer head stares out from a wall, cobwebs laced around its glass eyes. In the dark kitchen, a can of cranberry sauce stands alone on a shelf; the stove and oven lost in a corner. Billy Boy walks down a hall, the sound of each step filling the house. Suits and a hanger full of ties crowd a bedroom closet. A dresser stands beneath a mirror. Sheets and blankets on a bed as if just made. The smell of mildew hovers heavy as smoke. Only thing missing is Mr. Arthur. Billy Boy takes a couple of shirts and jackets. They'll go to waste if he doesn't. Mr. Arthur would want him to have them.

Sitting on Mr. Arthur's bed, Billy Boy looks out the bedroom window at a backyard sloppy with water from the recent rain. He remembers how thunderstorms flooded streets when he was a boy. He'd drag an old mattress from a trash pile and do somersaults into the water and play for hours. The sight of garbage reminds Billy Boy of home, makes him feel like an eight-year-old again. Much of the trash, he thinks, doesn't come from the Village. Contractors who won't pay a dump stop here and unload it. To Billy Boy, it's beautiful. He can hear his scrawny boy's body splashing in the stinky water with the funky mattress. He felt a kind of freedom. If he had an opportunity to go back in time and record it on camera, he would. He came up amid all this garbage and felt joy.

A homeboy, Sean, died in the yard next to Mr. Arthur's house. He had wandered around to the back and saw some guys he didn't like. They didn't like him either and started shooting, and Sean ran, falling beside a trash can. As he bled out, people

say he called for his momma. The guys who killed him dead
now too. Shot. What goes around comes around. Mr. John has
a photo of Sean on the Memorial Wall. Another homeboy died
on First Street not far from Hale Drive. He said something to a
dude that the dude didn't like. Bro what you say? and the dude
had a big-ass gun and shot him. Billy Boy didn't see it but he
heard the shot and was ready to throw down. If there's going
to be a war, me and my homeboy are going to win the war, he
thought, but that's not how it went. Homey died; war over, he
lost.

Billy Boy saw another homeboy get killed in front of a convenience store, Two Dragons. He tried to shoot a dude but his
gun jammed, and the dude turned around and shot him. That
was the first of many deaths Billy Boy witnessed. A bunch of
dudes chased another friend and shot him when he tried to
jump a gate. Not too long after that, Billy Boy hooked up with
two homeboys. They got carried away teasing each other; the
joking started getting personal. Went from laughter to serious
malice. Emotions got involved and then bullets flew and one
of them died. After so many years of killing, Billy Boy has no
expectations. He was exposed to death before he knew what
death was. Before he knew the word for it, people were dying.
He wonders when it will be his turn. He has been involved in
a couple of shootings but no one died. So many of his homies
have been killed that Billy Boy's like, I know I'm coming. Y'all
make some room for me in heaven because I know you're all
up there and there ain't no place else for me to go because I
know I'm coming. He has reached a point in his life that he
can't make friends because of love, man, because he loves so
hard. He's afraid he'll lose them. He tries to put restraints on
his heart and not feel. He considers himself one of the most

isolated people around. He doesn't really talk to nobody—no homeboys, no friends. No hee-hee, ha-ha, with anybody for real. It's too late in the game to play.

Billy Boy thinks that if people fought like the old guys did when they were young, the shootings would cease. But if a dude doesn't know how to fight, what're they going to do? They got a reputation to uphold. Imagine a guy with diamonds in his mouth, like Bigg Man, all beat up from losing a fight. He wouldn't be able to ride around all falsey like that without people laughing at him. So now when he throws down, he reaches for a gun. No one says, Hey man, remember when we went to school together? Remember when we played basketball at Light of the Village? No one says any of that. They shoot.

Billy Boy leaves Mr. Arthur's house. Knee-high grass brushes against his pants as he trudges through an empty lot. He considers himself a backstreet mover. He prefers paths and alleys in and around the Village instead of streets. Safer. If he sees somebody he doesn't know, he worries. Don't too many people move off the main roads. If it's an older dude, cool, but a young cat will make him paranoid. Why's he out here? Billy Boy has learned to be alert. Anything he sees that doesn't feel right or seems out of place arouses his suspicion.

Billy Boy was born in Sacramento but moved to the Village with his momma and grandmomma, Miz Annie, when he was five. Miz Annie grew up in Mobile and he presumes she wanted to come home. His daddy stayed in California but called every so often. Hey, his daddy would say, I'm going to mail you fifty dollars tomorrow. Then Billy Boy wouldn't hear from him again until the next time he offered to send money but didn't. His momma used drugs and would leave him in the house. I'm going out to eat, she'd say, and he wouldn't see her for weeks. But he'd die for her. Even though she wasn't there for him she's still his momma.

He relied on Miz Annie. She couldn't have been sweeter and gave him what she had even if it wasn't much. By-the-book kind of lady. She made sure Billy Boy attended school and showed respect. She was big on house cleaning. Chores and keeping the crib right. One time a lady made her so mad she tried to fight her from a wheelchair. Billy Boy laughs. Miz Annie could act crazy, man. Billy Boy called her momma. She died when he was ten, and Billy Boy moved from one auntie to another. He dropped out of school at thirteen and began hanging out with older cats and learned to sell drugs. Use your instincts, they told him. Follow your gut. Hesitate, you die.

Billy Boy feels the weight of the spirits of the dead like his homeboy Sean, and another homey, Cyrus. Billy Boy and Cyrus were thick as brothers. They protected each other. Watch-my-back-watch-your-back kind of love. One time as he sat in a car with Cyrus, a dude pulled up next to them and gave them a troubling look. Damn, Billy Boy thought, there might be some shit, and cocked his .45, but nothing happened and Cyrus pulled off and cruised to Burger King. At the drive-through, they asked for two Whoppers. Billy Boy reached into his pocket for change and nicked the trigger of his gun. *Boom!* The bullet went through the floor and into the front right tire.

We got to go, Billy Boy said.

Hell no, I want my food! Cyrus said.

Man, these people are going to call the police.

Not before I eat, Cyrus said.

They bought their food and limped off, the flat tire slapping the pavement. The police never did catch them. Those kinds of stories become legend in the Village.

Billy Boy decides to stop by the church. Hit up Mr. John for his birthday. He just wants a pair of kicks. Mr. John will understand. As he walks, Billy Boy remembers a recent dream he had about playing basketball with Cyrus. Then he dreamed about Sean. He asked him how death felt. Chill, Sean said. Billy Boy has been dreaming about dead people since he was little. He spoke to prison counselors about his dreams but they told him they couldn't provide the help he needed. After a while, Billy Boy embraced his dreams. They remain the one way he can still see dead friends, and they feel so authentic, man. In one dream he wanted to warn Cyrus he would get shot, but he didn't want to upset him. So Billy Boy stayed quiet and then, as in the real world, Cyrus died.

13

Jesenda considers returning to the church this evening with her children for the after-school program but decides to stay home and clean and wait for Melvin. She wants the house nice for him. She gets so busy she forgets to take care of him. He complains to her about that. You're always doing this with your family, or you doing something at the church. He has a point, but he hasn't supported her in the way she would like. He doesn't always respond to her in bed. I'm not with my family or at the church now, she told him one night, but he wouldn't touch her. He made excuses. I'm tired. She wonders if he has a girlfriend on the side.

Jesenda knew Melvin from the Village, where he also grew up. They dated when they were younger but split up. He had kids; she had kids. Then he and his babies' momma separated, and Melvin and Jesenda ran into each other at a laundromat. He asked her, When are you going to let me take you on a date? That's up to you and if your funds are good enough to take me on a date you can afford. They laughed. She put her clothes in the dryer and he walked over to help her. She didn't have enough money to dry them. I got it, he said. He sent her messages on Facebook but never asked her out. She invited him to dinner one Sunday night. They ate and watched TV and relaxed. He started stopping by more and more and it just pretty much went from there. He did what he had to do to keep her, and she did the same for him and thinks she still does. They supported each other in bed and out. He wasn't perfect but he wasn't bad, either.

They live in Mobile and rent a subsidized one-story brown house with a sloping roof. The dirt yard has only a few blades of grass. Their dog, Lucky, chained to a tree, barks at squirrels scattering fallen leaves. Collapsed bricks from a firepit Melvin built lie on the ground.

When she was growing up, Jesenda's auntie posted lists of rules throughout her house, and she has followed that practice. She has rules up in every room: Don't stand on the furniture. Put things away where you found them. Clean the dishes after you eat. No horseplaying. If you mess it up, you clean it up. No eating or drinking in the living room. Clean up behind you. Bathroom: You use it, you flush it. She can't stand walking into a bathroom and seeing one of her kids has not bothered to flush the toilet. Oh, she hates that. Bedroom: No jumping on the bed, no playing. Play outside and sweep up dirt you track in. Prince still jumps on his bed. But he behaves well in school.

New rule: If your woman takes care of the children, bring her flowers.

She maintains order so she won't be fussing all the time. She doesn't want to be the kind of momma who stays on her kids all the time. Yelling things like: Get out of the living room. Get off of the couch. Get out of the kitchen. Having rules helps. Her kids know what she expects. Her nephews and nieces too.

They call her the sign lady. She has posted rules in every house she has lived. Too many rules, her kids complain. Three weeks ago, she stood on the kitchen counter to put a light bulb in the ceiling and fell and busted her lip. Her left shoulder still hurts.

New rule: No standing on the kitchen counter.

All of her rules, however, can't improve the condition of her house. The landlord came over the other day to fix a few things but he didn't do much. Not really. Repaired a hole in the roof by putting a blue tarp over it, which wasn't repairing it at all. She can still see where the ceiling leaks. During a storm, the tarp collects rainwater and sags through the hole. He patched a hole in the wall with plaster but he didn't sand or paint it so that it would blend with the rest of the wall. It looks like a big, gray wart now, not presentable at all. Jesenda wanted another hole repaired, and the landlord said he'd send someone but they never showed up. Another person did drop by and glued a strip in the floor where her son kept tripping on loose tile but it popped up the moment the dude left. The kitchen sink leaks. She places a bucket beneath it every time she washes her hands. That annoys her. She pays for that wasted water. The people at the housing authority get on her for complaining. You can't tell us how to do our jobs. Hell, she's not telling them anything other than to fix things.

New rule: Don't move in to a Section 8 house with leaks, holes, and a bad roof.

It doesn't ever get easy, especially when times are tight. She just has to remain determined. What should she be doing differently? Is there something better than this that she's missing? Never get comfortable, she tells herself. Keep striving. She wants to do so many things besides her cleaning business. She wants to learn twelve different languages and travel the world.

She speaks only English and her speech isn't very polished. She doesn't know her multiplication tables, and she should if she wants to operate a business. Division, too. She would like to go to school again. No one took the time to teach her. Her momma and daddy died, and most of her foster parents wanted to collect checks instead of help her with school—and she wasn't the best student. Her social worker was a really caring person, but she didn't have time to teach her a lot of things. What she didn't learn from her auntie, she learned from her mistakes and she made many mistakes and still does. Like letting family live with her. Her light bill got up to $500 the last time her sister Kathy and her kids stayed with her for a few months. Hey, she said, can you give me fifty dollars on the bill? They got mad and left without offering her a penny. Makes her feel like an old lady.

New rule: Don't put up with family.

She remembers something Steve Harvey, the comedian and television host, said on the radio the other morning. Something like: You get eighty-thousand-some seconds a day. If there are twenty-four hours in a day, how many seconds in an hour? That's way too much math for her, but she hears what he's getting at: Every second of her life should count. She shouldn't waste them, but she does. Distraction and discouragement get the best of her sometimes. She doubts she'll ever earn $2,400 a month, for real. She tries not to be negative but she can't shake that sense of being stuck. High one minute, low the next. She thinks she and Melvin would be a whole lot happier if they left Alabama. Like a crab in a barrel living in Mobile.

14

Billy Boy reaches the church, walks inside, and contemplates the Memorial Wall. He sees the photographs of Sean and Cyrus, reaches out and touches them, stares at them a moment longer, then turns and walks back outside.

He sees Da'Cino and follows him to the Lighthouse where Mr. John sits on the porch swing. Billy Boy reminds Da'Cino about his birthday and asks him to hit John up for some shoes. Da'Cino walks up the steps. Billy Boy remains at the bottom.

Billy Boy wants to buy shoes for his birthday.

John looks around Da'Cino at Billy Boy:

How are you going to buy shoes without any money?

I don't know, man.

How much are the shoes?

Eighty dollars.

C'mon, Da'Cino, you know you're flush, John says.

Who?

You.

Man, I don't have it. I'm going to stand by the dumpster and smoke a cigarette.

That's where your money's going, John says.

Da'Cino makes a face and wanders back down the steps. John rocks back and forth, considers Billy Boy. Ten years ago, when Billy Boy was eighteen, John spoke by phone to his father in Sacramento.

I'm ready to be a dad, his father said. I want him out here with me. Can you do that?

Yes, of course, John said.

Send me a picture of him.

John did.

Oh, he looks great, his father said in another call. He gets that from me. Get him out here.

John and Dolores bought Billy Boy clothes, had a big send-off for him at the ministry and drove him to the Mobile bus station the next morning at eight o'clock. On the way home, fifteen minutes before the bus was to depart, Billy Boy's father called John.

I don't need him right now, he said. Better stop him.

Sir, he's got all his stuff and is really excited. He's at the bus station.

Yeah, well, I can't do it.

Nonchalant. No emotion.

Let me give you his number, John said, so you can tell him.

No, I don't want to talk to him. You call him and tell him. Click.

With only minutes remaining before the bus left, he tried again and then called Billy Boy.

Hey man, I just talked to your dad and he said he may not be ready just yet. Might need us to wait a little bit.

Oh, OK. Is that what he said?

Yeah, that's what he said.

OK.

Billy Boy didn't sound surprised, his voice flat. Another disappointment to add to a growing list of disappointments.

Can you pick me up?

I'll call your aunt.

She agreed to get him. She wasn't surprised, either.

What'd'ya think, Mr. John? Billy Boy says.

I'm getting ready to go pick up kids for the after-school program. What have you been up to?

Walking around the Village. It's my birthday coming up. Kind of special to me.

Yeah, John says, I know, but here you are.

I ain't in no trouble.

That's a plus.

I got nowhere to stay. I need a room.

Shoes and a room. What else?

Nothing, Billy Boy says.

Are you going to hang out while I figure out something for you, Billy Boy?

Yes, sir.

John stands.

I'm going to pick up the kids now.

Billy Boy walks behind him to the van.

Can I ride along?

Come on, John says.

Billy Boy opens the passenger door and gets in. John backs onto Baldwin Drive. Billy Boy stares out the window at the night sky alive with stars.

Somebody got killed last weekend.

Been a little shooting today, too, John says.

Got to be careful at nighttime. It's crazy. Do a lot of shooting from the bushes. After my birthday, I'm going to go out of town.

Where?

I don't know. Somewhere. Anywhere. Start over. Be something positive. I need work.

A birthday is a good time to get a new direction.

That's what Miz Dolores says. She gave me a good talk today. She'll tough-love you, man.

John picks up the children and drives back to the church. They pile out of the van and run inside and John follows them, while Billy Boy waits by the door. Minutes later, John walks out and waves Da'Cino over.

I got a hundred bucks. That should handle the shoes. I'll tell him and then you want to run him up real quick to the store?

Da'Cino gives him a look. He thinks John can be too nice sometimes, but he knows John sees potential in everybody. He won't ever say, You can't do that. When Da'Cino was still a boy John told him: You made it through so much, you can make it through anything in life. Put your mind to it. John knew Da'Cino had no support at home. Neither does Billy Boy.

If it wasn't his birthday, I wouldn't do it, John says.

Da'Cino shrugs and walk to his car. John knows he disapproves but what should he do? Write Billy Boy off? Say, I don't want you around here anymore? How would that help? Enabling, the textbooks call it. It's easy to sit at home and recite academic rules of social work about what should and should not be done. In the field, it's much harder to do. John deals with people, not words on a page. They aren't canned goods with a shelf life. Billy Boy certainly isn't the only one. Many people see the ministry as an ATM. His phone pings with messages starting early in the morning to late at night. Reading a text is much easier than listening to their spiel: How are you, Mr. John? So glad you and Miz Dolores are here. John doesn't need the small talk, the false praise. Get to the point: What do you need? The manipulation couldn't be more obvious but he gives them what they want. It gets exhausting saying no all the time. At some point, he'll cut off the spigot and Billy Boy will leave angry, hurt, and confused but not surprised, and that's sad too. It's just shoes. A fleeting moment of happiness. Why not? Enabling. That's a good term. John supposes it applies to him.

Go get you a birthday gift, he tells Billy Boy and hands him the money. Da'Cino will take you. Then we'll deal with finding you a place to stay.

Billy Boy looks at the ground. He rubs the back of his right hand against his forehead. The evening closes around him. He takes the money without looking up.

Y'all going to make me cry, he says softly.

I don't know about that.

Thank you, man.

Alright, Bo.

I love you, Mr. John.

We love you too, you know that.

15

Billy Boy leaves with Da'Cino. Inside the church, Dolores tells Morgan she heard two shots from the Donut Shop. We have a broken arrow, she says. Dolores and Morgan stand by the doors to prevent the children from going outside. Minutes pass without more shooting. John walks to Dunlap Circle. Quiet. No one about. All clear, he says into a walkie-talkie, alerting Dolores. At seven o'clock, the children leave, their mommas sit in their cars waiting, and they hurry, in case the shooting starts again. Kind of cool, John thinks, how calm we all are. Kind of sad too.

16

Two days later. Friday, March 12, 2021, a sunny morning. The vague sound of a car far off. Lisa McGuire walks past Bigg Man's house on her way to buy cigarettes from the Family Dollar in Chickasaw. She sees him outside his door and raises her hand.

Hey, she says.

Bigg Man nods. He calls Lawrence about ten thirty. What up, cuz? Lawrence is at work and can't talk long. When he gets off the phone, he walks inside a trailer to plug in a copy machine. His sister calls him about a half hour later.

I have to talk to you.

About what?

About Bigg Man.

———

Bigg Man calls Miz Phyllis most days, but he doesn't this morning. Had she done something to upset him? she wonders. Nothing she can think of. He's just running around and forgot. You know Bigg Man, she tells herself. She'll talk to him later and give him a hard time. C'mon, auntie, he will say. She can already hear him and laughs anticipating his excuses. She sits outside her front door to enjoy the morning and squints at cottony clouds. Do fat clouds mean rain? she wonders. Might be a nice day, might not. Never can tell. At ten forty-five a friend calls.

Have you heard?

Heard what? Miz Phyllis says.

I got something to tell you about Bigg Man.

What? The police done got him?

No, something badder than that.

—◆◆◆—

Miz Julia sees a young man in a hoodie running with a pistol. He turns down a cut into the Donut Shop. She hears gunshots and then sees the same young man running back through the cut. She doesn't know what he did, but she can guess. She sees young people toting guns and firing them off like it was nothing. When she was younger, the police would stop boys and search them. Boys didn't have no guns in them days. They used their fists or, like her daddy, a knife.

—◆◆◆—

Da'Cino is chilling on the front porch of his sister's home in Gulf Village when he hears gunshots from the Village. Not near but close enough. Moments later the scream of police sirens. Oh man, what's going on? Da'Cino wonders. I hope no one got hurt.

He thinks of Mayo. Da'Cino had been on D block when he heard the gunshots that killed him. He walked toward the noise and saw Bodine giving Mayo CPR.

He leaves his sister's house, sees the police converging on the Donut Shop and turns in that direction. He notices Bigg Man's red car and parks. People run past him and try to gather around it but the police have already cordoned off the area. Bigg Man's feet stick out of the passenger side, his upper body stretched out like he had been reaching for something near the steering wheel. Red sweat suit, white-and-red sneakers. Da'Cino sees the bullet holes in his back. His stomach twist into knots and a hollow emptiness consumes him until he doesn't know what to feel or how. He calls John.

———

In Bay Minette, Dolores hears the phone ring. John picks up.

It's Da'Cino, he says.

Oh, crap. Dolores thinks. At this hour on a Friday morning it can't be good.

Bigg Man, John says when he gets off the phone.

Nothing more. Dolores doesn't need more. She feels exhausted as if she hadn't slept, the morning assuming an unexpected weight. Everything off kilter. She knows what Da'Cino told John without knowing. She doesn't ask questions. He was Bigg Man; he was Corey. He knew his choices. For him not to choose to live a better life . . . She has no words. Thoughts fail her. Just the waste of life. It breaks her heart.

Bigg Man's murder surprises John and he feels a deep sense of despair that he always experiences when someone from the church gets shot, although Bigg Man's lifestyle made his death an almost foregone conclusion. He had known him since he was a child and he liked him, a lot, everyone did, or almost everyone. Oh, man. Oh, crap.

Someone will try to find who did it, maybe more than one someone. Battle lines will be drawn and pretty much anyone will be fair game. John wants to be able to say he did everything he could, but he wonders. People get killed and locked up, it's a reality, it sucks. Has he become too inured to the consequences of working here? Where are his tears? Where lies his grief?

John leaves for the Village. Dolores stays home. She seldom goes to murder scenes. At this point, all she could have done has been done. Corey is in God's hands now.

—◦◦◦—

John meets Da'Cino in the Donut Shop about about an hour after the shooting. Police try to shield the body from onlookers, but a man's angry shouting ignites the mostly young male crowd into a rushing surge against the officers. The scene becomes an unworldly chaotic roar of shouting, screaming, and sorrowful wailing. The crowd's agitation surges and subsides in waves until the police manage to surround the car and the coroner removes the body.

Da'Cino tells John rumors have already begun that one of Bigg Mann's homeboys killed him. Got into an argument and that was all it took. Everybody knows the dude.

Sad news, John texts the staff, *Bigg Man (Corey) was shot and killed in his car at the Donut Shop. Da'Cino and I are here and will keep you guys posted as we pray for his family and the community.*

———

Miz Phyllis cries, her voice rising in agonized keening. On the news, the police are calling one of Bigg Man's homeboys a person of interest. She knows him well. Why? Why? Why? He and Bigg Man were tight. They'd been hanging together three days before watching TV and just chilling. Bigg Man had taken homeboy to the mall and bought him clothes. Homeboy didn't have any money, and that was the problem. He asked Bigg Man to lend him a few dollars and Bigg Man said he couldn't do it. Not after he had just bought him clothes. That's what they got into it about, Miz Phyllis feels sure, her tears turning to anger. Money and clothes. Talking that mess, but Bigg Man wasn't scared. He didn't get scared. If he had his gun he might be alive right now. Homeboy knew he couldn't whoop Bigg Man so he snuck around a house and he shot him as he walked to his car. She thinks he didn't mean to kill him, just shoot him in the leg or something. Killing him was dumb luck and now he probably thinks he's a badass.

But he wasn't no killer, for real, until now. He's riding that coattail of being a badass, but he's no badass.

Why? Why? Why?

—◦◦◦—

Da'Cino's sisters ask him if he will post RIP for Bigg Man on Facebook. No, he tells them. No, no, no. He doesn't need to get caught in the middle of all that. He wants to avoid trouble, not be seen as taking sides. If someone asks him about Bigg Man's murder, he won't comment. He'll act like he doesn't know about it.

—◦◦◦—

John plans to hold a vigil for Bigg Man the following week but cancels it. The rumor circulating on the street is that his homeboys and those of his suspected killer intend to show up and shoot it out. People tell John they won't attend. He believes it gives too much credit to suggest that the opposing factions stand for much of anything but an addiction to drama and the adrenaline rush of confrontation. A twisted effort to assert themselves, a perversion of male pride. Their allegiances if any are shallow at best.

John brings a dinner of chicken, mashed potatoes and collard greens to Miz Phyllis and speaks to her and Lawrence about the threats. Though he has never canceled a vigil, they don't object to his suggestion. Sometimes people just sound off and don't do anything but sometimes they do everything he fears. He'd prefer to avoid any uncertainty than be stubborn and stupid. As a good friend from the New Mexico Military Institute likes to say, You only have to be wrong once for tragedy to occur, just not today.

———

Days later, Da'Cino sees someone driving Bigg Man's red car, the blood and stuff cleaned off. He can make out bullet holes. From that day or another day, he doesn't know.

———

Tommie Bonner bicycles down Baldwin Drive collecting cans. Crows fill the trees. They flew inside his building this morning. Two weeks ago he caught a wren in his rat trap. He felt bad about that. That durn trap has killed lizards, cockroaches, and a green frog. He picked up the frog and tossed it out to the birds. He stops for a can. He never knew Bigg Man and has no idea someone killed him.

———

On a Tuesday evening, during the after-school program, Lawrence tapes Bigg Man's photo to the Memorial Wall a little below the picture of TJ and next to the one of Corey Jr. Number forty-four. Miz Phyllis doesn't attend. The photo shows Bigg Man throwing a football, a red cap on his head, the bill turned backward. He wears a look of intense concentration as if transported to a stadium in front of thousands. The men, women, and children in the church celebrate Bigg Man as they knew him: the jokester; the boy who Miz Dolores told to bury his stolen shoes; the man who bought bicycles for boys and girls at Christmas. He had dreams. He had opportunities he didn't pursue, which everyone understands and takes from it what they will.

PART THREE

1

A spring morning not yet dawn. Little more than two years since Bigg Mann died. The street lights on Wilson Avenue dim against a filmy haze. A few parked cars against the curbs. Down darkened side streets house by house, frame doors loose on their hinges. Ripped screens scattered with bugs drugged motionless by the humid air. Too early for birdsong. A tension in the silence, a prelude to the gunfire that interrupts it. *Pop, pop, pop.* Then silence again for the briefest of moments before the sound of shouting, screaming. Dogs barking. The wail of sirens.

2

Miz Phyllis remembers:

One of her friends called her. You heard about it, didn't you? Heard what? Miz Phyllis asked. They got Bigg Man's killer. Miz Phyllis said, No girl. She didn't believe it. Then Lawrence called. Momma what are you doing? How are you feeling? I'm alright, Miz Phyllis said. Momma, you know last night someone shot the homeboy who killed Bigg Man. He got into it with some dudes. Lawrence couldn't have been happier.

Miz Phyllis got off the phone and stared at the floor. Justice had been delivered. She never wished anyone no bad luck, only justice for Bigg Man. The police never charged his homeboy with murder, but God charged him. Justice has been served. It was the best day of her life. Now, homeboy's family is going back and forth with members of her family on Facebook, swearing vengeance but it's done. They know what he did to Bigg Man. Even if they won't admit it.

Miz Phyllis knew homeboy's momma. They had been friends before all this. They were cool but God got everybody's time measured out. Out there doing wrong, you better do right or your clock is going to get punched. Bigg Man and his homeboy, two young men. Who is homeboy going to shoot now? No one. He's dead. God has seen to that.

She still misses Bigg Man. She liked to visit with him in the Donut Shop near a hit house and play dominoes, but the morning he died God didn't let her go that way. Instead she stayed home and had to call her sister, his momma, and tell her that the son she never raised had been killed.

The year after he died, she, Lawrence, and her daughter organized a memorial service. Memories were shared:

He loved cornbread. Whenever Miz Phylllis cooked anything, he'd say, You put sugar in it? You can put your own sugar in it, she'd tell him. He was like, I don't know what you be making but I'm putting some sugar in it. Sugar even in spaghetti. Some people eat it like that. Put it on like salt.

He knew all about cars.

He could throw a football like nobody's business.

Mr. John reminded everyone how Bigg Man helped the McGuire family. That was Bigg Man, Mr. John said. He wasn't perfect but none of us are. All of us have those special memories that can't be overshadowed by what happened. No more sorrow.

Miz Phyllis sighs. Bigg Man can rest. Homeboy can rest. He ain't got to run no more. Ain't got to hide from no one including himself. It don't matter how anyone else feels about it. It's over.

3

Miz Julia sits at a picnic table at Light of the Village. Tommie approaches her on his bicycle and stops, picks up a can, and drops it in a dirty sack suspended from the handlebars. The shallow morning light makes him squint. The wind carries trash and nudges the beer bottles he collects against the stones.

He applied for Social Security a few months after Bigg Man died and the agency approved his application. A check arrived for $2,300. He stayed in a motel for two nights to celebrate, soaking in a bath, watching CNN, and eating Hartz chicken. He thought his can-collecting days were over but his next check, arriving just four weeks later, was only $700. He didn't understand the cut and still doesn't. He called an 800 number repeatedly but no one answered. Morgan told him he may have been mistakenly approved for disability before the error was caught and that could be the reason his payments were reduced.

Tommie turns sixty-six in a few months. He worries if he rents a room and the Social Security office cuts his check again, he'd be back on the bricks again. With so much uncertainty he doesn't want to give up his spot at the academy. Some other

homeless person might take it, and then where would he be?
He applied for public housing but hasn't heard anything. A
lady at the housing authority told him she had worked there
for seven years and in her experience one-bedroom apartments
rarely become available. He feels stuck. Instead of renting a
room he'll use his check to stay in a motel two nights a month
to take a break from the streets. He misses Crichton. Those
were good days living with his momma.

—∿—

Tommie gets off his bicycle and sits across from Miz Julia.
   Hey, Miz Julia.
   Give me a cup of milk or a sandwich.
   Nope.
   OK, Miz Julia says. That's honest.
   I'm homeless, Miz Julia. What I got to give you?
   I heard you came into money.
   Tommie laughs.
   Did and until I didn't.
   Where's that trailer you were getting?
   Need money for a trailer, Miz Julia.
   Ain't got no milk?
   Nope, Tommie says.
   I ain't got a damn nickel in my house. When I came here I
was a working person.
   Hear about the shooting?
   When?
   Over the weekend.

Whoever it was had to be crazy.

Sure was, Tommie says.

He's dead?

Who?

I don't know, Miz Julia says. Someone always dies when there's a shooting. They all carry guns.

He's dead.

Whoever he was, he was stupid. A man got shot down the street on Dunlap.

The one I'm talking about was downtown.

Short skinny guy, light-skinned Black man about this tall he got killed. He wasn't but this tall. He'd get drunk and cuss you out. Better if you never spoke to him. He got shot three times.

That's a different shooting than what I'm talking about, Tommie says.

Which one are you talking about?

The one over the weekend.

What happened?

A man got shot. Why are you walking around with a pair of scissors?

I'm going to kill that boy staying with me. He took my only milk.

Come on, Miz Julia, Tommie says. You'll go to jail.

I don't care.

Well, you'll get plenty of milk and Bologna there.

I ain't playing. That boy staying with me took my goddamn food stamp card too. My memory is so bad I can't remember where I put it, so I gave it to him to hold for me. And he went to the store and bought himself all sorts of things. I want my food stamps back or he can get the hell on. I try to be nice and give him a place to stay and he does this. Worst mistake I ever made. All them canned goods, I lined them up on the table right where I sleep on the couch. SpaghettiOs and corn is gone. He took them too. I'll show him. My momma told me, You won't live past twenty. I'm seventy-four now. Momma called me evil. My momma's men would get so drunk they'd go to sleep up under the house after they were through with her. I never flip-flopped between men. I've gone through a lot in my life. My TV still works. It's the only company I have.

You don't have to put up with that, Tommie says.

I worked hard for my house. Why should I leave? I want to stay at my place. I paid for it. I paid for everything. I was in New York at a young age working. And Detroit. Came home to take care of my daddy.

Well …

The church is closed. Ain't nobody here to help me but you. If you got no milk and a sandwich, give me a drink of water, anything.

I ain't got it.

OK. That's honest. My daddy killed a man. If he was here, that boy in my house would be gone.

4

Da'Cino wakes up in the Lighthouse, shuts off his alarm, kicks out of bed, and gets ready for work at Chick-fil-A in Daphne. He showers, changes into a red polo shirt and dark pants. He clips on his name tag. Will have to pay the company six dollars if he loses it.

He left the church a few months after Bigg Man died. John and Dolores were cool. Do you like living in the Village? John had asked him. I like living in the house, Da'Cino said, but I don't like living in the 'hood.

You have to do what's best for you, John told him. We'll support you all the way, you know that.

He took a job at Walmart but didn't like it. He felt his coworkers screwed off. While he stocked shelves, they took long breaks but he caught all the flack. Hey, Da'Cino, you have to be proactive, his manager told him. He was like, What? These guys take two-hour breaks and you're coming down on me?

His coworkers made assumptions about him because he lived in Prichard and that bothered him too. A few of the women said, You don't seem like . . . and their voices trailed off. Seem like what? he asked them. You don't act like you're from Prichard. He didn't say anything to that. What was he supposed to say? Sorry, I'm polite? What does he have to apologize for? One of the women lives in Prichard and she wasn't at all like him. She cussed and got loud. He could be loud too, but joking to break the boredom. She said she knew him from Light of the Village but he couldn't place her. He ran into shoppers from the Village who remembered when he worked at the movie theater in Spanish Fort. You working here, they said? It embarrassed him, for real.

He knows John and Dolores will let him stay in the Lighthouse but he thinks he should move and start fresh. He's been dating a woman for about two years. They'd been coworkers at Wind Creek Casino and kept in touch. He stays with her in Atmore. He likes it there. Not much going on other than the casino but that's OK, although sometimes he wants more time to himself. She thinks he avoids her. Why don't you want to talk to me? It's not that I don't want to talk to you. I just want to be alone. She expects him to tell her everything, but he thinks she wouldn't understand.

Just the other day he was at his sister's house in Gulf Village talking, when *bam, bam, bam*! and she and Da'Cino dropped to the floor. She'd been trying to break up with her boyfriend and he got pissed, drove to her house and started shooting. A bullet struck the taillight on Da'Cino's car. His sister called the police, but when they arrived she lied and told them everything was cool. She said she thought she'd heard gunshots but it was just her boyfriend knocking on the door. The detectives never spoke to Da'Cino. If they had, he would have told them the dude shot his car and he had the bullet holes to prove it, but she is his sister, and the dude is her boyfriend. If she didn't want to tell the truth, the police probably wouldn't have cared what Da'Cino thought. His sister is just like his momma. Her boyfriend might as well be Joe. Those dudes can do whatever they want. Same as when he was a kid and his momma let Joe run over them. He feels bad for his nieces and nephews. They don't have a home, for real, when the adults around them all act like fools. It's broken.

He saw his birth father on April Fool's Day. Appropriate, he thinks. One of his sisters had a birthday celebration, and he showed up. He wanted to meet all the grandkids and have his kids from different women meet each other. He told Da'Cino he followed him on Facebook. Bullshit, Da'Cino thought. After thirty-some years, he just showed up. He never apologized for not being there or for saying Da'Cino and his sisters weren't his kids. Instead, he blamed Da'Cino's momma for his absence. Da'Cino no more believed that than he did the Facebook lie. I lived without you because you couldn't stand up to my momma? Get out of my face, man. If you followed me on Facebook you knew where I was, you knew I was with the church. If you wanted to get to know me, that's where I was. Nothing was stopping you from seeing me at the church. You had your chance.

He refused to speak to him. He knew if he said anything he'd cuss him out. His sisters called him daddy but not Da'Cino. He had not earned that right, not from him. Why did he wait this long to meet him? Maybe he was sick. Maybe he was dying. Da'Cino didn't care and neither did his momma. He tried to kiss her but she was busy drinking. He can't make up for all the years. Too late to throw a football together. Too late to help him with his homework. Too late to teach him how to drive. No time left for daddy-son things. Da'Cino is a grown man now with his own life. It is what it is. He won't be like him.

Da'Cino still can't get over Bigg Man's death. He feels vulner-
able having survived so long. Too many people he has known
are dead. Like he knows no one in the neighborhood anymore.
Nobody is around. They're gone. Dead and gone. He and
Bigg Man talked every now and then. They weren't tight, but
Da'Cino knew him. After he died Da'Cino saw his suspected
killer all the time. He walked around like he owned the street.
Da'Cino assumes the police didn't care about Bigg Man. Just
another dope dealer. Probably thought he was a target anyway,
and homeboy too. They were right. Now there are two fewer
people the police need to lock up.

Bigg Man never hung out with any one person. Da'Cino
would always see him with a bunch of guys. His killer was part
of the crew. He bit Da'Cino when they were twelve playing basketball. Hopped on his back, dug his teeth into him, and took
off running. Da'Cino chased him down the street but didn't
catch him. Homeboy came from a family with a little money
and always had new shoes. Bigg Man probably passed him in
the money game. That might be the reason homeboy shot him.
Out of jealousy. Da'Cino never thought Bigg Man would stay
in the game as long as he did. He lasted a good little while. He
always wanted to be rich.

Da'Cino recently turned thirty-one. He earns eighteen
dollars an hour at Chick-fil-A. His manager likes him because
he works fast, but Da'Cino doesn't want to be there. He feels
like working at Chick-fil-A is a step down from his previous
jobs. He started out as a general manager of a whole movie
theater when he was only a teenager. Now, he fries nuggets.
His life is moving in the wrong direction. Chick-fil-A is fine for
now but he has to find something else. He doesn't want to be
sixty-five and retire from Chick-fil-A. Hopes not.

5

Jesenda sits outside her house in her car trying to start it but the engine won't turn over. She can't imagine what's wrong with it. She has an interview for a truck-driving job. K & J something. Doesn't need a CDL, that's good. Pass a background check and she'll be good to go. The job starts at eleven o'clock, runs till about seven the next morning. Melvin will watch the kids and she'll be home in time to take them to school when he leaves for work. She hopes this job eases some of the stress at home. Melvin's checks don't cover all of their bills, car loan, and other stuff. If she starts making money, they can start saving and get out of Mobile.

She and Melvin are doing better. These days they argue without screaming. That's an improvement. Do you think we need relationship counseling? she asked him. How is someone going to tell me how to fix my relationship? he asked. If we can't figure it out, nobody can. OK, Melvin, whatever. He acts like he knows everything. Can't tell him nothing. He's never wrong. Even when he's wrong, he's never wrong. She won't worry about it. Her cleaning business died and she has too many other concerns to trip about him. Maybe Melvin had been right when he called it "little." It certainly never got big.

However, for a moment it looked like it might. She found work cleaning a Mobile apartment building a year ago and thought she had finally hit her stride. The manager and her husband had just bought the complex. I'm really just getting started, Jesenda told them at the interview. I've been up and running for maybe twelve months, mostly at a church. But I've been cleaning forever.

You sound just like my husband, the woman said. He's been doing roofing for a long time but he just started his own business. So he's doing the same thing you're doing, calling around, Hey, how are you doing? Do you need any roofing jobs done?

That impressed Jesenda. Like she wasn't alone. The lady's husband struggled too, and she'd compared her to him. Jesenda was like, Wow that's high praise. No one had ever thought so well of her.

My momma used to do the same thing, clean up, the woman said.

Wow, Jesenda thought again.

She got hired. Jesenda changed the name of her business to Just Send Her Cleaning, playing off her name. She thought it sounded more professional.

She cleaned seven units and more some weeks. Hey, Jesenda, the manager would say, we have a few apartments we need you to do a deep clean, can you put them in your schedule? Jesenda would do them all the same day. Some jobs only required her to sweep and mop. Other units needed the ceiling fans wiped down, the baseboards scrubbed, the windows washed. She felt sure she would reach her goal of earning $2,400 a month.

After a few months, however, the manager stopped calling. Jesenda would text her but she wouldn't respond. Finally, after a few days, she got back to her. She'd given Jesenda's hours to a friend who needed work. Like a slap in the face. That was a lot of money to lose. She still cleaned but not as often. Her pay dropped to $300 or less every two weeks, not enough money for a household with three kids and bills. Her friends told her it was better than nothing. It is nothing, Jesenda said, and quit

About the same time, Pee Wee, the father of her daughter Taylor, and a friend shot and killed each other in a drug dispute. Jesenda thinks there is more to the story. Doesn't make sense. They'd been friends for years. She just can't believe they'd shoot each other. She thinks a third person was involved. Pee Wee was twenty-nine.

Who expects anybody to die? No one, especially a child. Taylor doesn't have a daddy anymore. Jesenda can't call and ask Pee Wee to help her with the kids. Taylor saw him a lot. He'd been in her life. They were tight right up until he died. At least she'll have good memories of him.

Taylor bursts out crying when Jesenda least expects it. She tells her it's going to be OK. Her daddy is watching over her. He's her guardian angel now. When Jesenda lost her daddy, it hurt. When she lost her momma, it hurt even more because she had not recovered from her daddy's death. She knows Taylor's pain. Time won't heal it, but it will help her learn to live with it.

The loss of Pee Wee and her job sapped Jesenda's drive. Getting up every day and thinking, OK, I'm not on nobody else's schedule; I'm either going to find houses to clean or I'm not. It was harder than she'd anticipated. She knew what she should do but didn't have the energy. She worried about Taylor. She had to help all three of her kids with their homework and cook and clean the house for Melvin. She lacked motivation to do more.

Eventually she took a job at Walgreens for twelve dollars an hour. She enjoyed working the front register and meeting people, but the manager always made her clean the bathroom, which she didn't appreciate. She quit four months later but found a job at Alabama Cleaning Service for $9.50 an hour. Less than Walgreens but still a job. She established a routine: Drop the children off at school, get to work by eight, , punch out at three, pick up the kids. On slow days, she'd sit in the janitorial closet and nap. The company had a break room but no one could find her in the closet. It was a big closet and another lady slept in there too. Jesenda liked working again but quit after a few weeks. The pay was too low and not worth the effort. Her friends tell her she can't keep jobs. I can, she tells them, but I want something I like. It bothers her to be an employee when she knows she could work for herself if someone gave her a chance.

She hopes the truck-driving gig comes through. Keep focused, she tells herself, but staying focused is hard. She thinks of Bigg Man and her cousin, Lil Joe. He's dead now too. Just twenty-four years old. Shot on Wilson Avenue. He talked about driving trucks just like Bigg Man. Real estate, too. He thought he might get into that. Not anymore. His funeral program said he graduated high school and attended Light of the Village as a boy. That was it. Jesenda worries that little more will be said about her when her time comes.

She knew the dude everyone thinks killed Bigg Man. She never had no problem with him. He took a break from the streets, got him a job in construction and said he didn't want to be out there no more. He was doing well until other people pulled him back into the life. Once you're in the streets, it's hard to leave. Like drug withdrawal, for real. Jesenda is glad she outgrew being crazy. She doesn't have time. But other people, they do so much street stuff that when they leave it no one believes them. Everybody considers them gangsters and won't let them be anything else. A lot of people say, You're a product of your environment, and Jesenda believes it. As long as you stay in that environment where can you go? Her son Prince asks her questions every time someone gets shot. Are they dead? He called one shooting victim his big homie. Prince is too young to really understand. Taylor feels sad for the kids. She's still getting over losing her daddy. Well, that's the lifestyle they chose, Jesenda tells her. Lil Joe, Bigg Man, Pee Wee, and people like them, you can expect their lives to be short. Only three ways out of the Village: walking, driving, or flat on your back.

She and Melvin still hope to move. His kids live in Mississippi and Florida. They visit in the summer. It would make sense to be near them. Both states are close to Alabama. Easier than moving to California. All kinds of places they could go but no one ever leaves. Not that she's seen. It's not really nothing ever new, just a different generation that stays stuck. Maybe she and Melvin will break the cycle. First she needs a job. It hurts her head thinking about it.

6

Billy Boy roams the cuts and switchbacks, crashes with a cousin some nights when he doesn't seek an empty house in the Village. He ain't trippin' off Bigg Man and whoever shot him. If it was who everyone says it no longer matters. They're both dead. Full circle. They made their choices. When you've only lived one way, the vision of a different life stays too blurry to believe. Like a mirage. It seems impossible, for real.

Billy Boy reads the Bible. He believes God sends him subliminal messages. God communicates through symbolism because he ain't going to come straight down from heaven and talk to Billy Boy. He allows Billy Boy to have visions. Billy Boy waits for a sign. He tries not to think about it too hard or he might miss it.

Whatever someone does out here in the Village gets done by choice. If they sell dope, then it ain't like someone forced their hand. Wasn't like their momma wouldn't buy them nothing. It ain't about that. Selling dope was something they wanted to do. Don't do anything stupid and then fall on your knees and ask God for help. At the same time, Billy Boy wonders, How do you tell a guy he can be this or that if he has never seen it, never heard it, and his role models are dope dealers and prostitutes and killers? Every homeboy he knew who died in a shooting could have been one of the best at something. Billy Boy doesn't think about them too much unless he's with somebody and they mention them. What can he say? Nothing. They're gone.

It does something to his heart, deaths back-to-back-to-back. He worries about dying. It makes him take life seriously. Maybe his fear is not for himself but for the people he cares about. The not knowing what's going to happen to them, thinking they might go before him, increases his loneliness. How old is he now? Thirty. Can that be right? He has survived this long but expects no celebration.

7

John walks behind the ministry and crosses Dunlap to the Donut Shop. He glances at the streetlights. Been out forever. It's little things that show decline. Trees cut, and the city leaves all the limbs at the side of road. Looks like crap.

He enters the Donut Shop and absorbs the quiet. Young men used to fill the area like a packed stadium. When he and Dolores started the church, he would see cars all around the hit house here, the empty homes nearby frantic with activity. Trap houses, people called them, places to hide drugs. No one stole another's stash because someone would rat them out and lethal repercussions would follow.

Silence hovers over everything now like a shroud. A few squirrels and the passage of a crow but no other sound. The police cleaned everyone out after Bigg Man died. Cars, boom boxes, benches, folding chairs, all gone. John thinks he should call it something else. A donut shop never closes. Sure feels closed now.

The entire Village may become just as quiet. The Alabama Department of Environmental Management found that Prichard's aging water system, particularly in the Village, has so many leaks and other problems brought on by decay that it costs the Water Works and Sewer Board approximately $222,000 a month, or nearly $2.7 million per year, in lost revenue. Some city officials support a plan to shut off service to the Village, condemn the properties, pay the owners, and find alternative homes for renters.

John knows Light of the Village may have to move, he knows, but it won't close. He believes it has helped reestablish community in the Village, a symbol of faith, hope, and love in the most dire of circumstances and should be allowed to stay. However, none of that may matter to the officials who will decide its fate. Worse comes to worse he and Dolores will relocate to another part of Prichard. They'll stay and not abandon the families they have known for two decades. More than enough people have done that.

In the meantime, he deals with the day-to-day. Shootings continue. Since Bigg Man died, twenty-six names have been added to the Memorial Wall. Death can happen so fast. Some kid steps on another kid's shoe and tempers jump from zero to sixty in seconds and if it doesn't result in violence, that's a blessed day. Usually, the explosion happens faster. Onlookers egg them on. People start texting, Hey, somebody laid their hands on your little brother, and his family will show up just like that.

John has never seen anyone beaten up. Not bad anyway. Teenage boys just shoot one another. Little kids up to fifteen, they'll scrap, but it doesn't end there. The worst thing that can happen is if a kid wins a fight. The onlookers post it on Facebook and the loser feels humiliated. So they go home and get a gun.

Bigg Man never did take John and Dolores out to dinner. John has no doubt he wanted to. Just one of those things that slipped by. John can live with that. In many ways Bigg Man's death is a story that has been told many times, but each version is different and each person is different. He was more than a statistic, more than a number. When John thinks of him, he sees the boy who carried off a cake from a restaurant buffet. He always had a young face, a kid's smile. Had he put his mind to it, he probably would have been a good truck driver.

The family paid for a horse-drawn carriage to haul his coffin to Old Plateau Cemetery in the historic Africatown district of Mobile. Handpicked flowers of all colors clutter the cross above his tombstone. An engraving shows him throwing a football. *In Loving Memory to Corey Davis. 1995–2021. Long live Bigg Man. Bigg on Bigg.*

When John sees the kids of Bigg Man's alleged killer at the church, he steers clear of any mention of Bigg Man. One afternoon some of the other children started making fun of them. We know what your daddy did. John told them to stop and changed the subject by making a joke. You're trifling, he said, Y'all so trifling, something the kids tell him. Don't be trifling, Mr. John. They laughed, got distracted, and stopped their teasing. Two families, two sets of kids without fathers. Bigg Man's people feel avenged. A rough justice.

John knew the homeboy everyone assumes killed Bigg Man but not well. He was likable but always different. Very deliberate, direct, mature in a hard sort of way. Like Bigg Man, he had his followers. He participated in the lives of his children. Not much but more than most.

Back in 2012, a shooting on Hale Drive wounded three young men who had participated in church activities as boys. John drove to USA Health University Hospital in Mobile, where they were being treated. One of them was Bigg Man's alleged killer, then fifteen. He had been shot in the abdomen. A doctor asked John to talk to him. The injury was not life-threatening, but the boy was hyperventilating and the doctor worried his anxiety would lead to cardiac arrest.

Can you calm him? the doctor asked.

John stepped over to the boy's bed and held his hand and stood where he could watch the blood pressure monitor. The ceiling lights bore down. God loves you, John said. You're going to live; you have a purpose. He stayed for two hours until the boy relaxed.

In June 2020, the boy, now a young man of twenty-two, drove to the church to wash his car. By then he had a reputation of running in the streets. John saw him and stopped to talk. He'd always wondered what it took to live that kind of life and decided to ask him.

What do you have to do to be successful in the Village? John said. Do you work with other people, trust them?

The young man cut him off.

You can't trust anybody, he said. Not when money is involved.

That was the last conversation of any length John had with him. They took a photo together. John is wearing his sunglasses and sports a lopsided grin. Homeboy is smiling, his right arm draped around John's shoulders, his chin jutting up in the air.

What's up, Bo? John shouts to a man peering out the door of a ruined home.

He doesn't answer. A dog barks.

John feels the space left vacant by Bigg Man's death. People with big personalities are missed more than others. Not long ago, John saw a funky dude who looked like Mayo from a distance. Wow, John thought, there's Mayo. Well, wait a minute, no he's not. Recently, Jamez told him he could still see Mayo's face.

John hates telling sad stories, but people in the Village do die. The lives of the men, women and children on the Memorial Wall have something to say. Should he keep that a secret because they ended in tragedy? Every donor wants to see a return on their investment, see that bar graph rise twenty percent. That's why movies in which the kid beats all odds do so well. A good film financially, but not one hundred percent accurate.

It would be great if Jesse Darrington graduates from college. If he and his two brothers make it as society defines making it, that would be wonderful. That would be really cool. They survived some major crap. He'll see how it goes for them. Jesse has enrolled in engineering classes and showed John his grades, B's and C's. He acts like it's no big deal. He seems to be doing well. He doesn't hear from him much. He has a girlfriend. Leaving Gulf Village was a good thing. Tragically, he and his brothers had to lose their mother to do it. Whatever her faults, she stayed vigilant with her children and would be proud of them now. She instilled the drive to succeed in each one of them.

It amazes him what the Darrington brothers and so many other children have lived through. One kid got shot and thought it was hysterical that the bullet struck his funny bone. He'd hidden under a house, a dog cowering beside him. He laughed about that too. His aunt came to the hospital and wanted to look at the wound. She lifted the blanket. Hey, wait a minute, auntie, the boy said. I ain't got nothing on under there. He was released that night and now lives a good hour away from the Village. He works security and stays out of trouble. He and Jesse. Two good stories. Da'Cino, that's three. He spends most of his time at work or in Atmore. John wants Da'Cino to have more of a future than a fast-food restaurant can provide. Of course he has to earn money, but it's weird he doesn't see his potential beyond the immediate need for a paycheck. He has achieved more than most of his friends and siblings. Maybe that's enough.

John sees Light of the Village as a family, supportive but challenging like a family should be. Dolores and Morgan have asked Da'Cino, Why aren't you studying for your GED? but he's shown no interest in trying again. Maybe they expect too much. Da'Cino has come a long way. He never pursued the street life. Maybe that's success enough. Should he have children, perhaps they will want an education and a career that meets someone's standards of success.

Jesenda has dropped out of sight, and Billy Boy asks for money. He has squandered so many options. John feels sorry for him. He never had a steady place to live, kicked around from one relative to the next. He could probably do something productive—or maybe not. Dolores would give him jobs but he wouldn't complete them. Said his hand hurt.

John follows a road out of the Donut Shop. The wind stirs, the air damp but warm, sunlight peeking through clouds. A stop sign on a street named Madison Avenue carries graffiti: *PA for Life*. John thinks it means Prichard, Alabama, for life. Like a prison sentence. There had been houses all the way through here at one time. Nothing now except the rusted frames of stolen cars.

A kid named Elijah lives with his grandmother around the corner, another boy, Daniel, nearby. He would come to the ministry with Elijah. Elijah's aunt brought them but Daniel hasn't been around for a good while. A dude called "Diamond Dog" lives not far from here. He serves as the Village mechanic.

John remembers one boy, about twelve years old. He injured his arm playing football but the family wouldn't take him to a doctor. They told John they wanted the disability check. Everyone called the kid "Chicken Wing," because his arm was noticeably deformed. It would have been an easy fix. An orthopedic surgeon who volunteered at the church examined the boy. How long has it been like this? he asked the family. Well, it's been a while. It will have to be broken and surgically reset, the surgeon told them, but he's young enough it should be fine. They never did it. The boy died in a car accident.

No one believes John when he tells this story. They accuse him of attacking poor people. He's not attacking anyone. He heard them with his own ears. He's not saying the members of that family are bad people, but but he can't help but still be shocked skewed thinking, the desperate things people do to survive. What died in them that they would see a child as a means for a check? But it's taboo to talk about it. People condemn what they do not understand and use it as an excuse to avoid the Village. Avoidance does not give anyone the moral high ground. They want a long Shakespearean tale to give meaning to tragedy, but one doesn't exist. Tragedy has no need for embellishment. The Village does not exist in another world but in this one.

John keeps walking. He follows a street through all the overgrowth toward Bigg Man's house. He last saw him here early on a sunny morning two days before he died. Bigg Man had been up and busy, everyone coming around. Cars idling out front for only one reason. Got to get it. Early bird snags the worm. Bigg Man held a shoebox where he kept his money, or so rumor had it. Rode around with it too. Didn't leave it at his house, a pre-caution against burglars. He leaned into the passenger window of a car the metal studs on his white belt catching the sun. After a short moment, he jogged into his house.

What's up? John called to him. It's early, Bo, too early to be up.

Big Man glanced at him and kept moving. He wasn't playing.

John smiles at the memory. He recalls the early years of the church. He and Dolores were suspect then. Everyone was friendly but people did wonder about them. After twenty years, a few still do. Other people, too, wonder. Some of them think he and Dolores want to save souls and charge their egos. If anyone thinks they drive home at night feeling empowered, they don't understand, they really don't. Most days John feels deflated. It sucks caring about people who self-destruct. Sucks big time.

It should be me up on the Memorial Wall next, he has said more than once in Bible study. At fifty-eight he is much older than the young people staring back at him, but he knows the chances of him dying before any of them remain slim. A child or a young man or woman will beat him to it. An argument over a girl, someone feels insulted, a robbery gone bad, or something equally stupid will result in death.

Most days John feels immense joy and immense sorrow and not in equal measure. He and Dolores get through their days by staying focused on their mission: Show love, hope, and faith. Let the Bible speak for itself; see who it touches. Listen, encourage. Be present, consistent, and genuine. Tell the truth in a kind way. Don't condemn or judge. Help in whatever way possible. Be present. That man, woman, or child you see today may be dead tomorrow. Or sooner. Suck it up. Know you're doing everything you can. No life is cheap. But it can be short. He knows of only a few second chances.

John and Dolores fall back on scripture: "The King will reply, 'Truly I tell you, whatever you did for one of the least of these brothers and sisters of mine, you did for me.'" Find the Jesses, the Da'Cinos, and the Jesendas; the Billy Boys, the Mayos, the Josephs, the Coreys, and so many others. They're all different. They all have equal merit.

John tells anyone who will listen, If you feel compassion for someone, don't ignore it, explore it. You don't have to go all Mother Teresa and run at full speed, but you can investigate it, search for it.

Who do you feel compassion for?

What moves you?

Whose life can you touch?

The answer, he believes, is a gift from God.

Light of the Village Memorial Wall

1. Trayon Jeffers   June 6, 2009
2. Sean Cook   March 15, 2010
3. Cyrus Singleton   August 26, 2010
4. Taneja Wilson   October 3, 2010
5. Tyre "Rude" Robinson   August 7, 2011
6. Marion "Bad Baby" Miller   October 8, 2011
7. Keonte "Kelo" McCants   November 29, 2011
8. Tony "TJ" Brisker   December 21, 2011
9. DeVontae "Vontae" Purifoy   April 18, 2012
10. George "Plies" McGee   August 18, 2012
11. Detoria Cook   September 11, 2012
12. Marchellis Moran   November 11, 2012
13. Jodeci "Gucci" Woodard   May 15, 2013
14. Shadarrius "Redd" Moffett   October 9, 2013
15. Anthony "Head" Carstarphan   February 22, 2014
16. Santrez "Romey" Hunter   May 3, 2014

17. Canzio "Red" Robinson — November 13, 2014

18. JerMichael "DBO" Anderson — June 29, 2015

19. Donald "DJ" Coleman Jr. — December 12, 2015

20. Kaylieb Gatson — January 3, 2016

21. Demetrius "Blood Raw" Brown — January 26, 2016

22. Deshawn Jones — January 26, 2016

23. Trenholm "Trent" Rice — September 24, 2016

24. Ricky "Bookie" Hill — November 25, 2016

25. Robert "Boomer" Howard — December 16, 2016

26. Jeremy Jones — January 9, 2017

27. Marion "Mayo" Awudu — February 12, 2017

28. Henry King — October 7, 2017

29. Carlos "CJ" Peebles Jr. — October 19, 2017

30. Cindy Darrington — December 1, 2017

31. Demetrius Robinson — April 21, 2018

32. Ricky Glenn — October 12, 2018

33. Xyadarius Harrison — November 10, 2018

34. Antrell "Bam" Nichols — January 5, 2019

35. Maurice T. Jackson — June 13, 2019

36. Dorne "DJ" Wheeler Jr. — June 15, 2019

37. Corey Davis Jr. — January 30, 2020

38. Arthur Williams — February 5, 2020

39. George "Boo Face" Paige III — February 7, 2020

40. Joe Locke — June 20, 2020

41. Shameka Dees — July 7, 2020

42. Sara "Ms. Jean" Mosley — September 10, 2020

43. Lamar Miles   September 13, 2020
44. Roslyn "Cooney" Agee   January 22, 2021
45. Corey "Bigg Man" Davis   March 12, 2021
46. Terrance Hill Sr.   August 13, 2021
47. Joe "Lil Joe" Johnson   October 10, 2021
48. Kyng M. Lyons   February 3, 2022
49. Roderick "Black" Stewart   February 9, 2022
50. ReShaun "Pee Wee" Cunningham   May 10, 2022
51. Joseph "Trey" Jones III   May 10, 2022
52. Trey Norwood   May 17, 2022
53. Ni'Kiyah Lucy   May 24, 2022
54. Anthony "Lil Ant" Greene   June 4, 2022
55. Carlnelius Harris-Porter   September 1, 2022
56. Ja'Mil Dwayne Autry   October 3, 2022
57. Jonathan Higgins   October 15, 2022
58. DeCisco "Cisco" Tillman   December 4, 2022
59. Jaylin Foxx   February 19, 2023
60. Kenneth "KP" Poellnitz   March 7, 2023
61. Donnie Williams   April 29, 2023
62. Jacquell "Joc" Graham   May 14, 2023
63. Victor "Vic" Miles   May 28, 2023
64. Darryl "Dman" Moffett   June 2, 2023
65. LeCharles King   June 18, 2023
66. Nathan "Nate" Harbin   June 28, 2023
67. Lakeva Latasia "Keke" Dees   July 31, 2023
68. April French   May 12, 2024

69. Asa Jones   June 30, 2024
70. Zeke Cano   October 6, 2024
71. Ammie McGinney   March 7, 2025
72. Frenicka Craig   April 17, 2025

Acknowledgments

To the people of Alabama Village: You welcomed me, a complete stranger, into your homes and gave of your time even when it was inconvenient and when my questions required you to relive painful memories over and over again. You taught me much more than I could convey here, and were patient, honest and courageous. I am humbled and grateful for your generosity and trust.

Specifically, I want to acknowledge Phyllis Davis, Da'Cino Da'Marcus Dees (my boi!), Betty Catlin, Lil OG Catlin, Jamez Montgomery, Julia Gordon, Lawrence "LRG" Davis, Jesenda Brown, Aaron "Billy Boy" Amison, Daniel "Dee Tee" Tillman, Joseph Torres, Tommie Bonner, Patricia "Pony" Hayward, Deborah Lacey, Paul and Lisa McGuire, Tyra Quinie, Jesse Darrington, and many more than I have space to mention but please know you have my heartfelt thanks and appreciation.

I also want to acknowledge the staff of Light of the Village for everything you did to make this book possible. My thanks to John and Dolores Eads, Morgan Copeland, Janie Widemire, Jordan Crane, Kristen Jordan, Elisabeth Davis, Erica Barksdale and Julisa Theodore.

288 Alabama Village

My thanks to William Kinnaird, George Kennedy and Robert McClendon who gave generously of their time and insight.

Special thanks to Susan Curtis, Roland Sharrillo and Bruce Janssen for reading early drafts of this book. Also my thanks to the editors at *Wrath Bearing Tree* for their support and encouragement of this project.

My thanks to Dan Simon and everyone at Seven Stories Press for taking this book on.

Finally, I want to acknowledge Corey "Bigg Man" Davis: You more than contributed to the education I needed to proceed with this book. I'm sorry you're not here to see it.